PRAISE FOR VALLEY SPEAK

"I wish I had written this book. With it you'll be able to convince anyone that you're a Silicon Valley insider." — Guy Kawasaki, Chief Evangelist, Canva and former Chief Evangelist, Apple

"The speed with which technology created in Silicon Valley has changed the world is well known. The Valley's unique and fast changing vocabulary should be equally well known and understood. This book makes it easy and fun for the reader to understand, catch up and hang on as Silicon Valley surges ahead." — William H. Draper III, General Partner, Draper Richards, and Author, *The Startup Game*

"If you're new to Silicon Valley, get this book!" — Jager McConnell, CEO, CrunchBase

"Kopp and Ganz have crafted a Rosetta Stone for all those entrepreneurs wanting to decipher the lexicon of Silicon Valley and increase their chances of getting their startup funded." — Jay Samit, serial entrepreneur and Author, *Disrupt You!*

"With Valley Speak, anybody can 'fake it' in Silicon Valley." — Dan "Fake Steve Jobs" Lyons

"As Silicon Valley has become, even more than in the past, the leading global center for technology, innovation and entrepreneurship, interest is exploding in how it works. Valley Speak provides a valuable and entertaining guide to the terminology, and ultimately to the thinking, that connects Silicon Valley's players with each other, and increasingly with the world." — Sean Randolph, Senior Director, Bay Area Council Economic Institute

"Valley Speak finally brings some clarity (and a nice dose of humor!) to all the fancy jargon. Think of it as Webster's dictionary for the Valley." — Jeremy Cotter, President, YouRockThis.com

"Valley Speak is a very timely book as I find myself explaining many of these terminologies to people that are not based in the valley. Rochelle and Steven not only provide a definition, but context, examples and quotes. A great read that can help you carry more meaningful conversations in Silicon Valley!" — Anish Srivastava, Founder & CEO, Vinaj.com

"Valley Speak is an invaluable read for all those new to the Silicon Valley world—I wish it had been around when I started MOVE Guides in London in 2011" — Brynne Herbert, Founder & CEO, MOVE Guides

VALLEY SPEAK

SPEAK

Deciphering the Jargon of Silicon Valley

ROCHELLE KOPP and STEVEN GANZ

VALLEY SPEAK
Deciphering the Jargon of Silicon Valley

Rochelle Kopp and Steven Ganz
Genetius Publishing
Redwood City, CA

Copyright © 2016 by Rochelle Kopp and Steven Ganz

Genetius Publishing books are available at special quantity discounts to use as premiums and sales promotions, or for use in educational or corporate training programs. For more information please email us at publishing@genetius.com or call 650-260-2031.

Cover and interior illustrations by Sergio Garzón
Cover design by Pixel Studios
Interior design by Davis Creative, www.daviscreative.com

Although the author and publisher have made every effort to ensure that the information in this book was correct at press time, the authors and publisher do not assume and hereby disclaim any liability to any party for any loss, damage, or disruption caused by errors or omissions, whether such errors or omissions result from negligence, accident, or any other cause.

Publishers Catalog In-Publishing Data
Kopp, Rochelle, 1964- | Ganz, Steven, 1966-
   Valley speak : deciphering the jargon of Silicon Valley
   Library of Congress Control Number: 2016906847

   Redwood City, CA : Genetius Publishing, [2016] | Includes index.
      ISBN 978-0-9974364-1-9 (Ingram Spark hardback)

      1.) Business enterprises—California–Santa Clara Valley (Santa Clara County)-Terminology. 2.) High technology industries—California–Santa Clara Valley (Santa Clara County)-Terminology. 3.) Microelectronics industry—California–Santa Clara Valley (Santa Clara County)-Terminology. 4.) Jargon (Terminology)—California–Santa Clara Valley (Santa Clara County)

   LCC HF1002.5 .K66 2016 (print)| DDC 650.014--dc23

| Printed in U.S.A.

To Lyssa,
who never made it to Silicon Valley

Table of Contents

Preface

Break shit ... unicorns ... pivot ... monetize ... growth hacking ... People from other parts of the country love to hate the way that people in Silicon Valley talk. The region's unique business culture seems to breed new words—cool, geeky, and often inane words—that, like the Valley (as it is affectionately known) itself, beckon popular participation but somehow simultaneously create an aura of impenetrability.

Yet with the area's vaunted success, interest in the Valley and its culture has grown enormously. Regions around the world look to replicate the Valley's success, both from the top down via government support and from the bottom up as individuals act more entrepreneurially. Firms based in other parts of the U.S. and overseas have developed relationships with Silicon Valley companies large and small as well as with other institutions, such as universities, based here. Many firms have already set up outposts here.

When we moved to Silicon Valley, we found it challenging to pick up the lingo, even though one of us has a Ph.D. in Computer Science and the other has an MBA. Around here, people toss off sentences like "Everyone thought that semantic search startup launched by those Stanford whiz kids was going to be the next unicorn, but now they are doing a down round and it's looking like they are candidates for an acqui-hire." It can be awkward if you're the only one who doesn't understand what people here are saying.

In her work with clients from Japan (and other countries) doing business in Silicon Valley, Rochelle discovered that they, too, often have difficulty understanding the various unique terms used here. This led to the idea of creating a book deciphering Silicon Valley vocabulary, and in June 2015 we published, in Japanese, *Silicon Valley Buzzwords*. While working on that project, we discovered that there was no book in English on this topic ... so we decided to create one!

We believe that the best way to understand Silicon Valley is to learn its vocabulary. Knowing the local jargon will enable you to foster and enhance relationships with the people who work here, think along the lines of firms that have been successful here, and further explore the rich history of Silicon Valley and the colorful personalities who have built it. The words we present in this book are carefully selected to help you to understand the processes of technological innovation—including the funding and development of startups—that are so central to the Valley. Learning these terms will bring you "up to speed," whether you're planning on doing business here or just want to understand the latest episode of HBO's *Silicon Valley*.

Since varying definitions of the area exist, we should say what we mean, specifically, by Silicon Valley. The term is still generally used to describe the area southeast of San Francisco, extending from Redwood City to San Jose and typified by Palo Alto and Mountain View. The culture of Silicon Valley has spread so thoroughly, however, that the label now often refers more broadly to the entire San Francisco Bay Area. We also recognize that this culture and its associated lingo have already spread, to some extent, to many areas outside the San Francisco Bay Area and even outside the United States.

We see this book being of interest to those coming into contact with this area or its culture and wanting to better understand it. But we also see it being of interest to those already here. We cover a lot of material. Those familiar with any one part might be less so with another. Silicon Valley often asks or requires us to wear multiple hats.

The book is divided into eight thematic parts. We begin by discussing some of the characters that one may encounter in the Valley. We then talk about various aspects of business in the Valley—startup funding, innovation, product development, recent key technology trends, marketing, and human resources. Finally, on a somewhat lighter note, we present some of the lifestyle quirks that are prevalent here and will likely soon reach *your* area, if they have not already arrived.

Each of the book's over 100 chapters focuses on one word or phrase. Chapters begin with a short essay describing the use of the term, its relevance, and perhaps a bit of its history. Of course, many more than 100 terms are essential to Silicon Valley, so other related words are introduced, as appropriate, within these essays (marked in **bold**). *Italicized* words are introduced in other essays. We hope that even if you are generally familiar with a given term, our descriptions will give you some deeper understanding and insight. Below the essays are several sample sentences showing how these terms might be used in Silicon Valley. Each chapter concludes with several quotations, often from well-known Silicon Valley personalities, that provide further examples of use as well as often pointed opinions on the subject at hand.

While we stand behind the descriptions presented in the essay text, the example sentences should be considered as perspectives that one may encounter in Silicon Valley, along the lines of what one might overhear at a cocktail party. Of course, the quotations express only the views of their respective authors. Overall, the text is intended to present the diversity of views on its subject matter, some of which may be controversial, especially among Silicon Valley insiders.

This book may be read cover-to-cover, but that is certainly not required. The structure should tempt you to look up terms of interest and then jump to other words as they are mentioned in the write-up (the index should prove helpful for this purpose). We do not say that the chapters are independent—language is always interdependent—but the best entry point is the one that captures your attention.

Not everyone is thrilled with Silicon Valley and the way things are done here. They may be annoyed by the perceived smugness, sanctimoniousness, and self-importance. Or they may not like the prospect of losing their white collar job and replacing it with a gig economy position as a taxi driver (at the beck and call of an app and soon to be replaced by an autonomous vehicle). The fact that the language here seems designed to exclude others is in itself a turnoff as well. We hope that this book will help to open up the lines of communication, enabling a more robust and inclusive debate and keeping as many people as possible on board the fast-moving train that is Silicon Valley.

Perhaps to an even greater extent than Wall Street, Silicon Valley is subject to ups and downs. As this print goes to press, there is a lot of talk about a chillier environment for startup funding. But that doesn't mean that innovation here will grind to a halt. In Silicon Valley, a downturn is but a time during which massive development projects take place in scruffy garages rather than chic offices, setting the stage for the good times to roar back in with the next cycle. The language is a product of both the ups and the downs, as well as of the volatility, so this book will discuss both unicorns and unicorpses.

Rochelle has worked with many co-authors in the past, but this is the first time she has co-authored a book with her husband Steve. We certainly engaged in some heated debates on how best to explain certain concepts, but we are happy to report that our marriage survived this project. We enjoy exchanging our different perspectives—Steve as a computer scientist and startup founder and Rochelle as an MBA and management consultant—and hope some of that comes through and helps to clarify how people in Silicon Valley talk about business and technology.

We would like to thank several people. First and foremost, we would like to thank Eiji Doi, a leading figure in the Japanese publishing industry, who originally encouraged Rochelle to write about Silicon Valley's unique vocabulary. We appreciate the efforts of our able researchers: Teresa Dentino, Vincent Michael Leoni, Steve Newman, Paula Pastuskovas, Ryan Pfeiffer, Don Schroeder, and Whit Spurgeon. Thanks also go to Stuart Shea and Whit

Spurgeon for their skillful editing and for ensuring that this book made sense to readers outside Silicon Valley. And a special thank you to Deb Aoki, Adam Galper, Michi Kaifu, Guy Kawasaki, Anurag Mendhekar, Hiroshi Nozawa, Donald Olgado, Steve Omohundro, Warren Packard, Mary Russell, Carol Sands, Reuven Shelef, Tomohito Shimizu, Donald Steiny, Boris Strongin, Olga Strongin, Steven Telleen, Tatsuki Tomita, and Ben Zimmer—most current and former residents of Silicon Valley who suggested valuable improvements to the manuscripts of this or the previous Japanese edition. It's the smart and interesting people like you who make living here so stimulating. Of course, we take full responsibility for any remaining errors or omissions. We would also like to give a special thank you to the Unicorn level supporters of our Kickstarter campaign for this book: Harriet August, Leonard and Roberta Ganz, David and Jackie Kopp, Robert and Joann van Loon, NTR Lab, and Reuven Shelef, and to all of our other Kickstarter supporters, without whom this book in its current form would not have been possible.

Rochelle Kopp and Steven Ganz
Redwood City, California
May, 2016

Quick-reference Guide

The book is divided into eight thematic parts. Within each part there are multiple chapters, each devoted to a specific term or concept.

The first instance of each chapter name is **bolded** within that chapter. Other related notable terms and concepts are also **bolded** when they are first or most prominently introduced. All these terms are *italicized* when they appear in other chapters of the book, except within the example sentences and quotes. Hyperlinks in the e-book version connect all bolded and italicized instances of each item.

Links to the source web page for each of the quotes in the book are gathered in a special section at the end of the e-book version. Readers of the print version who would like to receive a document with the links should contact the authors (see contact information at the back of the book).

A complete list of the words discussed in this book can be found at https://www.wordnik.com/lists/words-covered-in-valley-speak--deciphering-the-jargon-of-silicon-valley. If you have suggestions for words that don't appear here that you would like to see us discuss in a future edition of this book, please add it to the list at https://www.wordnik.com/lists/suggested-additional-words-for-valley-speak.

THE PLAYERS

Startup

To many, a **startup** is just a new small business. While a small business may be content to remain small, however, a startup intends to grow into a large company. Startup *founders* are driven to create something that impacts their industry or market in a significant way.

A startup is searching for a *disruptive* **business model** (framework describing the business' operations and how they make money) that repeatably and *scalably* achieves **product-market fit** (delivers *value* to *target* customers). A key word is "searching"; a startup's model is unproven and its market uncertain. Because their offerings are speculative, startups have a high failure rate.

Hewlett-Packard, an early Silicon Valley startup, was founded in a garage in Palo Alto. Such rags-to-riches tales of great institutions emerging from humble origins inspire many *entrepreneurs* to attempt, sometimes successfully, to achieve similar extraordinary feats.

A key event providing impetus to the blossoming of startups in Silicon Valley was a 1957 dispute between William Shockley, Founder of Shockley Semiconductor, and eight of his employees, which led to their leaving to form Fairchild Semiconductor. Over time, Fairchild employees left to start their own companies, forging a chain of startup creation that continues to this day. Notable among those were Robert Noyce and Gordon Moore (the latter renowned as author of *Moore's Law*), who went on to *co-found* Intel Corporation. Likewise, Xerox's Palo Alto Research Center (PARC) has spawned numerous companies including Adobe and 3Com, the latter by Robert Metcalfe (of *Metcalfe's Law* fame and co-inventor at PARC of Ethernet). Its influence on Apple Computer's *user interfaces* is legendary as well.

During the dot.com boom of the late 1990s, excitement about new business models and an influx of *venture capital* spawned the next stage of startup growth in Silicon Valley. The business possibilities created by technological advances such as the mobile Internet have led to the current startup boom.

Example sentences:

He had a string of startup failures before hitting the mark with this last company.

Their startup is actively seeking investment from VCs.

Startup offices have sprung up in the recently gentrified area.

Quotes:

"A startup is a company designed to grow fast. Being newly founded does not in itself make a company a startup. Nor is it necessary for a startup to work on technology, or take venture funding, or have some sort of 'exit.' The only essential thing is growth." — Paul Graham, Co-founder, Y Combinator

"Over the last few years we've discovered that startups are not smaller versions of large companies. The skills founders need are not covered by traditional books for MBA's and large company managers." — Steve Blank, Author, *The Startup Owner's Manual*

"A startup is a fundamentally different kind of business than 99.9% of the businesses in the world." — Jack Menendez, Manager, Redheeler Software

"We learned to ignore the noise coming to us from everywhere, the noise of the startup ecosystem—we stopped calling ourselves a 'startup', a meaningless word that comes with too much baggage." — Rafat Ali, Founder & CEO, Skift

Founder

A **founder** envisions something great but lacking in the world and then takes the crucial next step of creating an organization to make it a reality. A founder often starts a company in order to manifest his or her idea, initially assuming all risk and reward. When several people unite to start a company, they are known as **co-founders**. Between co-founders there is a sharing of ownership, the percentages determined by mutual agreement. While the occasional *startup* is launched by several more-or-less equal co-founders, more commonly there is a key, initiating founder, with the remainder of the **founding team** referred to as co-founders.

There is also a legal difference between **founder's stock** (which gets a more attractive *vesting schedule* as well as *acceleration of vesting*) and other *restricted common stock*. Key people who are brought on board early in a company's development will often be called co-founders and given the benefit of founder's stock. Other human resources engaged at that time or later would be categorized as either employees or contractors.

Some *entrepreneurs* are hesitant to bring in co-founders because doing so means sharing ownership of the company. Well-chosen co-founders can, however, complement a founder's existing skills by covering the gaps, thus presenting a more robust set of capabilities. Many *venture capitalists* have a preference for funding a founding team rather than a single founder, because they consider a single founder to be a higher risk.

A founder seeking co-founders would be well-advised to begin by conducting a thorough and honest self-assessment of both proficient skills and deficits. Then, with the right alchemy in mixing skill sets and egos, you and your co-founders could become the next legendary Silicon Valley success story.

Example sentences:

The co-founders of that company are in their late twenties.

I was talking with the founder just the other day.

After a dispute with his co-founders, the entrepreneur thought it best to start over with an entirely new idea.

Quotes:

"One of the perks of being the founder is that you get to build the company in your image." — Mitch Kapor, Co-Chair at Kapor Center for Social Impact

"Look—this is the terror of being a founder & CEO. It is all your fault. Every decision, every person you hire, every dumb thing you buy or do—ultimately, you're at the end." — Ben Horowitz, Co-founder & General Partner, Andreessen Horowitz

"If you want (low) six figure salaries as co-founders—entirely appropriate once you are a 'real' company—then you need to raise $2m+, not $500k." — Jason M. Lemkin, Managing Director, Storm Ventures

"Nevertheless, VCs often drag their feet, waiting for the market to show them something, waiting for the founder to prove something or waiting for some demonstrable proof of value." — Phineas Barnes, Partner, First Round Capital

"As a founder you have to build a team some day, so why not start the day you found the company?" — Ron Conway, Co-founder, SV Angel

Hacker

In the most common Silicon Valley usage, a **hacker** is anyone who loves to push the envelope of what is possible within a system, most often a computer system. This may involve writing or modifying computer programs or making creative customizations to or combinations of computers and electronic equipment. The verb **hack** means finding a clever solution to a problem, often by modifying something in an original way to suit a convenient but unintended purpose. A related term is **mod**, a shortened form of "modification" or "modify". As a noun, **hack** can have a partially derogatory connotation of a quick-and-dirty solution that avoids the work involved in rethinking a design, similar to **kludge**. "Hack the ..." refers to finding a clever way to fix a broken system from within; in these cases, such as "hack the government," there can be practical impediments to changing the system through normal channels and processes. Hackers are likely to congregate at *hackerspaces*.

In the media, the term "hacker" is often used more narrowly to refer to those who apply their skills to infiltrate and wreak havoc on computer systems. The term **hacktivist**, a combination of words "hacker" and "activist," refers to people who break into computer systems for a politically or socially motivated reason.

Hackers of the first variety complain righteously about the hijacking of their moniker, and refer to individuals who find ways around security protocols as **crackers**. The term may denote only *black hats* with ill intent or those donning hats of any shade, but either way is generally pejorative. It's said that hackers build things while crackers break them.

In fact, both uses of "hacker", as well as the individuals described by it, have tended to walk a fine line between the playful and the malicious (as, perhaps, does human nature itself). All human progress begins with denying the inevitability of the constraints that confront us, but endeavors to overcome them can serve any purpose. Before there was Apple Computer, co-founders Steve Wozniak and Steve Jobs performed **phone phreaking** using a tone-roducing **blue box**, which made free calls by exploiting bugs in the design of the telephone system. Such activity had been referred to as "hacking" as early as 1963.

Example sentences:

Hacking a Wii console to control a model airplane resulted in an early version of a drone.

They encouraged a group of hackers to try to find flaws in their security product.

Hack the Hood trains low-income youth of color in technology and marketing skills.

Quotes:

"As any hacker would attest, when someone describes a challenge as impossible, you're motivated to prove them wrong." — Dan Guido, Co-founder & CEO, Trail of Bits

"Hackers don't take realities of the world for granted; they seek to break and rebuild what they don't like. They seek to outsmart the world." — Sarah Lacy, Founder & Editor-in-Chief, *PandoDaily*

"There are hardware hackers, people modding everything from boards onward to create performance or tools not intended by original manufacturers." — Daniel Kennedy, Chief Internet Security Officer, The 451 Group

"If you give a hacker a new toy, the first thing he'll do is take it apart to figure out how it works." — Jamie Zawinski, Proprietor, DNA Lounge

Whiz Kid

Every culture needs heroes, and brilliant engineers are the heroes of Silicon Valley. As a result, a variety of terms have come into use to describe the different types of technical geniuses that power innovation in the Valley.

Whiz kid is the designation bestowed on a young (generally under 25 years old) engineer or other specialist who has superior capabilities. Two other terms commonly used to refer to extremely talented employees, regardless of age, are **ninja** and **rockstar**. Software Engineer Jon Moter explained the popularity of these somewhat overblown terms as follows: "Maybe 'cause most of us engineers are/were big geeks, and like the idea of being bad-asses. 'Even though I didn't have a date to my high school prom, now I'm a ninja rockstar!!'" **Guru** differs slightly from these in connoting in-depth knowledge. These terms have begun to make an appearance as formal (although somewhat tongue-in-cheek) titles at many Silicon Valley firms.

Some say that an extremely capable programmer is capable of doing the work of 10 regular programmers; hence, another slang expression—**10x** (pronounced "ten-eks")—has emerged to refer to such individuals.

Silicon Valley firms' eagerness to hire these extremely talented individuals has resulted in a so-called **war for talent**—an extremely competitive environment for recruiting and retaining talented employees. This "war" has led to the high salaries and lavish *perks* commonly offered by Silicon Valley companies, as well as the practice of **poaching** (hiring away) prime employees from competitors.

Example sentences:

The latest whiz kid to receive venture backing is only 13 years old.

He's such a rockstar that he has offers from Google, Facebook, and Apple.

In her salary negotiations, she benefited from the raging war for talent.

Quotes:

"Engineers have very serious bullshit detectors. If a guy calls himself a ninja or a Jedi, he'd better be damned good." — Mike Sienkowski, Founder, BirdDog

"Great companies are built by great teams, so naturally, when it comes to technical talent, companies are competing harder than ever to entice the best of the best. The rationale you'll typically hear is along the lines of 'a great developer is 10x as productive as a mediocre one.' That might be true, but it is an impractical startup hiring strategy." — Avi Flombaum, Dean, Flatiron School

"This is why Silicon Valley's War for Talent hasn't always been good for the talent. After all, the only way to get much better at your craft is to be challenged in ways that make you uncomfortable. Yet not many people in high technology are uncomfortable these days." — Glenn Kelman, CEO, Redfin

"Geeks are a critical driver of America's innovation ecosystem, from the entrepreneurs launching startups in Silicon Valley to the scientists experimenting in university research labs to the whiz kids building gadgets in their parents' garages." — Todd Park, Technology Advisor, The White House

Geek / Nerd

Geeks and nerds—those who are unfashionable or socially awkward but smart and possessing a lot of in-depth knowledge about technical subjects—rule the earth in Silicon Valley. Indeed, much of the Valley's optimistic spirit is based on **technocentrism**, the idea that we can solve any problem by applying the right technology. For a group likely to have suffered ridicule in school, their prodigious and sometimes obsessive knowledge of an intellectual topic, especially in technology, has given them wealth, status, and power they likely never dreamed of.

Geeks and nerds are considered to differ in subtle ways. **Geeks** may be more outgoing, especially with respect to their more narrowly defined areas of interest. Geeks may be highly respected by those who share their interest, or denigrated by those who do not. But in Silicon Valley, pretty much any narrow interest has its following. To **geek out** on a topic is to explore it in excruciating detail. **Nerds** have more generalized high intelligence. They tend to be proficient in more abstract areas such as math and science in which the general population is not so well-versed; between this and their deficit of social skills, people may have difficulty relating to them. Fortunately for them, abstract knowledge is broadly applicable—nerds may be particularly well-suited to the fast-growing area of *data science*. Nerds are sometimes considered to be on the autistic spectrum, and indeed, Silicon Valley's incidence rate far outstrips other areas of the U.S. "Half of Silicon Valley's got mild autism, they just avoid the labels," says Temple Grandin.

Many view being a geek or nerd as a point of pride. For example, *VC* Dave McClure lists "Geek" as the first of several descriptors on his LinkedIn title. *GeekWire* and *GEEK* are technology news sites and Geeks on a Plane is a tour designed to help *startups*, investors, and executives learn about high-growth technology markets around the world. Nerd Night Silicon Valley is an event site catering to nerds and "Talk Nerdy to Me" has become a *meme*.

Example sentences:

The geekiest guy in our class is now the CEO of a giant software company.

My co-workers have lots of geeky hobbies, like flying radio-controlled helicopters and building robots.

The restaurant was full of nerds, celebrating the funding of their data analysis startup.

Quotes:

"Many start-ups are saved from disaster only by replacing the founders (geeks) with professional managers. Those managers, of course, must learn to work with geeks." — *Schumpeter* Blog, *The Economist*

"It is a common but incorrect myth that Silicon Valley is bro culture. Silicon Valley is geek culture, and we are the bro's natural enemy." — Marc Andreessen, Co-founder, Andreessen Horowitz

"If you like nerds, raise your hand. If you don't, raise your standards." — Violet Haberdasher, Author, *The Secret Prince*

"I know: I am a freakish geek. Or is that a geekish freak?" — Kara Swisher, Co-founder & Co-executive Editor, *Re/code*

"I want to tell any young girl out there who's a geek, I was a really serious geek in high school. It works out. Study harder." — Sheryl Sandberg, COO, Facebook

"I coined the word technocentrism from Piaget's use of the word egocentrism. This does not imply that children are selfish, but simply means that when a child thinks, all questions are referred to the self, to the ego. Technocentrism is the fallacy of referring all questions to the technology." — Seymour Papert, Co-founder, MIT Media Lab

Angel Investor

In the world of *startup* financing, there is a gap between *friends and family* and *venture capital*. Here flies the **angel investor**. While *venture capital* investments are typically nothing less than $1 million, a typical angel investment can range from a few thousand dollars to the low millions. Angel investors may take *convertible notes* or participate in a *seed round*, among themselves or alongside a *VC*.

Stemming from a term used originally on Broadway to describe wealthy theatre patrons who invested in productions, the term "angel" crossed over to the *startup* in 1978 when first used by the academic William Wetzel. At that time he had completed a landmark study on how *entrepreneurs* raised *seed* capital and began using the term "angel" to describe those investors who provided early-stage backing. The term stuck and angels continue to bless the most promising *founders*.

The typical angel investor is a wealthy individual, often someone who has been a successful *entrepreneur* themselves. They differ considerably in sophistication and will each look for different things in *founders* and ventures. *Crowdfunding* sites such as AngelList have opened the world of **angel investing** up to many more potential investors.

The risk for an angel investor is extremely high, as a large percentage of early-stage *startups* fail. In addition, angel investors do not obtain the benefits of diversification offered by *VCs* to their *limited partners*. Like *VCs*, angels often look for investments that can return at least ten times their initial investment, but their near-term goal is often to pass the company along to a *VC*, who will provide the capital needed to take it to the next level, with the angel staying on for the ride.

Example sentences:

Angel investing is a nice hobby for the semi-retired, post-exit founder.

When the former entrepreneur tried angel investing with the proceeds of the sale of his company, he realized that *identifying* a successful entrepreneur is quite a different skill than *being* one.

It would have taken all the angel investor's time to schedule with every entrepreneur requesting to meet over coffee.

Quotes:

"Angel investors also often want to contribute more than money to a young company. Angels have the experience, and inclination, to be great mentors and valuable directors." — Basil Peters, Author, *Early Exits*

"I only look at two things when angel investing. Are you solving an important problem? Do you care about the end users?" — Gary Vaynerchuk, Co-founder & CEO, VaynerMedia

"As an angel investor, the deal breakers for me are overly confident management, all male executives, [and] no sense of social give-back from the company founders." — Susan McPherson, Founder & CEO, McPherson Strategies

"The idea is that angel investors are supposed to be wealthy people supporting people who need funds, typically who are not wealthy, and don't have the ability to do it themselves." — Jason Calacanis, Entrepreneur & Angel Investor

"The key to making money in angel investing is saying no. You meet with 100 companies and say no to 99 of them." — Kevin Rose, CEO, HODINKEE

Venture Capitalist

A **venture capitalist (VC)** is a professional who invests third-party funds in early stage companies. This contrasts with an *angel investor*, who typically invests their own funds. Venture capitalists invest capital in these companies in exchange for an ownership position in the firm and its potential financial gains. The venture capitalist is primarily using monies from its accredited or institutional investor clients, which it amasses into a pool of capital called a **fund**, typically structured as a limited partnership. These investor clients are thus known as **limited partners** and, in this context, the VC as the **general partner**. A single fund may invest in as many as 20-40 *startups*. The limited partners share in the gains and losses. Limited partners generally promise their capital for only a limited amount of time, such as 10 years. The general partner is entitled to a fixed percentage of profits (known as the **carried interest** or **carry**), which they can take as *exits* close. But if the profit level is not maintained through future *exits*, the limited partners are entitled to **claw back** (require the return of) enough early profits to bring the general partner into compliance.

The venture capitalist might work independently or as a partner in a **venture capital firm**, for short a **VC firm** or just **VC**. Money raised from a VC firm is referred to as **venture capital**. Only a general partner has decision-making authority; *entrepreneurs* are initially more likely to interact with a VC firm's **associates**. Some VC firms use contracted **scouts**, often *founders* of former *portfolio companies*, who are compensated with a stake in the investments they recommend. At one time, venture capitalists were mainly specialized bankers. Now people go into VC firms straight out of school. Also, some *serial entrepreneurs* have emerged as venture capitalists, leveraging their hands-on, operational experiences.

VCs need to maintain both good relations with their *portfolio companies* as well as a degree of objectivity. Straying too far to the former is referred to as **going native**.

It is easy for *founders* involved in *pitching* to forget that *VCs* are also selling them and that a show of enthusiasm may be just that. Perhaps reluctant to curtail their options prematurely, a *VC* (or any potential investor or acquirer) may employ a tactic aptly (from the *founder's* perspective) known as **SHITS—Show High Interest Then Stall**.

Example sentences:

The VC had a full day of networking and meetings to review pitches.

Several venture capital firms passed on that deal and regretted it later.

They were dying to get their first meeting with a VC.

Quotes:

"From the outside or from what one reads in the blogs, these things may seem like shotgun weddings, but in reality, Big VCs 'track' potential investments and founders that catch their eyes for months and months." — Semil Shah, General Partner, Haystack

"While the investment decision is critical to portfolio performance, VCs spend more than 60% of their time on post-investment activities in order to grow investments for lucrative exits. These activities can be separated into monitoring (protecting the interests of the investor) and value-adding activities (strategic influence, mentorship and access to networks)." — Keet van Zyl, Co-founder, Knife Capital

"Venture capitalists historically have been the 'entrepreneurs behind the entrepreneurs' (quoting Sequoia) with a disposition to match. Specifically, venture capitals were usually nearly invisible to normal Americans and adverse to a high profile. It was primarily a cottage industry that preferred obscurity." — Keith Rabois, Investment Partner, Khosla Ventures

C-suite

People in Silicon Valley often chatter about the **C-suite** of a high-flying *startup* or established public company and the various **C-level** executives who comprise it. The C-suite refers collectively to the cherished C-level positions within a firm—ones that have titles starting with the letter C (for 'Chief'). C-suite thus refers to the executive team of a company, comprising those deemed to have the most power and influence in the organization. **CxO** refers to any member of the C-suite.

Typical C-level roles include the following:

- **CEO—Chief executive officer** (ultimately responsible to the *board of directors* for the success of the firm)

- **COO—Chief operating officer** (in charge of the daily operational functions of the company)

- **CFO—Chief financial officer** (responsible for monitoring and maintaining the company's financial situation)

- **CTO—Chief technology officer** (sets and conveys tech strategy)

- **CIO—Chief information officer**

- **CMO—Chief marketing officer**

- **CPO—Chief people officer** (or **chief human resources officer**)

CxOs exist in traditional businesses as well, but amid the proliferation of *startups* in Silicon Valley, anybody can be a CxO. In Silicon Valley you may find more CTO's than elsewhere, as the chief technology officer has an important role to play in companies focusing on technology development. Truly tech-oriented Silicon Valley cOmpanies are likely to have a **chief architect** (not of the form CxO), who is more narrowly focused than the CTO on standards for and evolution of current product offerings. It's also fashionable in Silicon Valley to make up C-level titles. For example, a "chief privacy officer" is now part of the executive team at Facebook. Many firms now have chief security officers as a result of the crisis in *cybersecurity*. Vint Cerf holds the title of Chief Internet *Evangelist* at Google. Pivotal Labs and Khan Academy have chief happiness officers.

Example sentences:

Her dreams of entering the C-suite were realized when the CFO stepped down.

Reaching the C-suite may mean a corner office ... or an upgraded beanbag chair.

Several of the firm's C-level executives had risen through the company ranks and knew all aspects of the business.

Quotes:

"It is all corporate Kindergarten playtime title-making. Most of these vanity titles don't even report to the CEO. The only C's with "real" power are the CEO, CFO and, occasionally, COO." — Mark Stevens, Author, *Your Marketing Sucks*

"The role of the CEO is to enable people to excel, help them discover their own wisdom, engage themselves entirely in their work, and accept responsibility for making change." — Vineet Nayar, Author, *Employees First, Customers Second: Turning Conventional Management Upside Down*

"Your game plan to present yourself and your product to C-level executives— CEOs, CIOs, COOs, CFOs, CMOs—is a completely different beast from an ordinary sales strategy." — Peter Daisyme, Co-founder, Host

"The first thing that always comes up when you want to discuss the role of a CTO is that there is no well established definition of what a CTO actually does. The role is very different depending on the type of company and the role technology plays in the company." — Werner Vogels, CTO, Amazon

Board of Directors / Advisory Board

Startups that incorporate may form "boards" of two varieties. Every corporation has a **board of directors (BoD)**, but **advisory boards (BoA)** are more likely to be found in Silicon Valley than in other places, and LLCs may form only this latter variety. Unqualified references to **the Board** should be understood to indicate the board of directors.

Advisory board members are often *thought leaders*. While individuals may be placed on an advisory board primarily for the value of their endorsement of the firm, smart *entrepreneurs* make good use of this resource, keeping members "in the loop" and looking to them for guidance. Advisory boards may convene as a group or merely serve as a collection of individual consultants to the *founder*.

The primary difference between the two kinds of boards is that a BoD, in selecting the *CEO*, has supreme power over the direction of the company; a BoA, by contrast, has power only through the strength of argument. While BoA seats are apportioned on the basis of merit or reputation, BoD seats are generally granted as a condition of investment. In fact, the distribution of BoD seats is a prime issue for negotiations between company *founders* and *VCs*. BoD seats may be dedicated to the *VC*, to the *founding team*, or to the *CEO* (often initially the *founder*). Because the BoD is a voting body, an odd number of seats is customary in order to ensure decisive action; *VCs* and *founders* can achieve this by assigning an **independent seat** subject to their mutual approval. Investors from prior rounds or junior *VC* reps may sit in on selected proceedings as nonvoting **board observers**. Also subject to negotiation is the degree of free rein given the *CEO*—the forms and sizes of transactions not requiring approval. BoA members may also receive *equity*, but a much smaller amount and generally subject to *vesting* on the basis of time or achievement of *milestones*. Active members of either board may receive cash compensation in addition to *equity*. Any board should have a clear understanding and agreement with the *founder* on its responsibilities.

Founders should choose their board of directors carefully, since it can replace them as *CEO*; *founders* should also humbly keep in mind that at some point that may be the best course for their company.

Example sentences:

The startup was thrilled to get their industry's prime thought leader on their advisory board.

The founder regretted selecting her for his board of directors when she voted to remove him as CEO.

When the CEO became embroiled in a scandal, the BoD decided to replace him with the COO.

Quotes:

"Fire Bad [Advisory] Board Members: If you realize you've made a bad choice, get rid of him or her. Unlike a board of directors, advisers can be replaced without a lot of legal headaches." — Geri Stengel, President, Stengel Solutions

"Startup founders often don't form a Board of Directors early enough. Board members can provide experience, contacts, oversight, and discipline. They can see the forest while you are looking at the trees. They can help you to avoid problems, and if that fails, help get you out of them. But this is a serious commitment; board members should allocate 250 hrs/yr." — Carol Sands, Founder, The Angels' Forum and Managing General Partner, The Halo Funds

"Personally, I think the ideal board structure for most early-stage companies is a 5-member board with 2 founders, 2 investors, and one outsider. I think a 4-member board with 2 founders, 1 investor and 1 outsider is also good (in practice, the even number is almost never a problem)." — Sam Altman, President, Y Combinator

Entrepreneur

An individual who continually identifies needs or wants and gathers resources to build organizations or initiatives around satisfying them—in spite of naysayers and the risk of failure—is considered an **entrepreneur** in the truest sense of the word. The product or service created by the entrepreneur need not be in technology and he or she need not seek a profit; it can be any organized endeavor to do something not done before... to create, to innovate, to change the world. While *founder* expresses a role in a particular *startup*, "entrepreneurship" refers to the corresponding state of being, and "entrepreneur" to those who exhibit it.

The economist Jean-Baptiste Say, as an admirer of Adam Smith's *The Wealth of Nations*, adapted the French term "entrepreneur"; he felt its typical meaning of "adventurer" described the essence of enterprising businessmen. Entrepreneurs create new markets and new opportunities; hence there is plenty of adventure in dealing with the unknowns of those situations. There is also speculation that the French were inspired by the Sanskrit word *antara prema* which means "inner calling." Do we glamorize entrepreneurs too much? Some in the world of *social entrepreneurship* think so, blaming such **heropreneurship** for a plethora of leaders and a dearth of followers.

In Silicon Valley *startup* culture, certain *founders* will create multiple ventures in succession with continued zeal to change the world. Their vision doesn't simply end with one adventure. These **serial entrepreneurs** continue to come up with new ideas and start new businesses. In perhaps the ultimate expression of entrepreneurship, **parallel entrepreneurs** start two or more *startups* simultaneously. Clearly these individuals have an endless supply of good ideas and incredible drive to succeed. Parallel entrepreneurship can make economic sense for the *founder*, who can spread the risk among various entities instead of betting everything on one enterprise. Some *VCs*, however, will suspect that they are spread too thin.

Example sentences:

The room was full of hoodie-wearing entrepreneurs.

Being pre-disposed to solve problems, engineers may have a leg up in becoming entrepreneurs.

She was a natural entrepreneur, constantly looking around the corner towards the next big thing.

Quotes:

"The critical ingredient is getting off your butt and doing something. It's as simple as that. A lot of people have ideas, but there are few who decide to do something about them now. Not tomorrow. Not next week. But today. The true entrepreneur is a doer, not a dreamer." — Nolan Bushnell, Founder, Atari, Chuck E. Cheese, and BrainRush

"I'm convinced that about half of what separates the successful entrepreneurs from the non-successful ones is pure perseverance." — Steve Jobs, Co-founder, Apple Computer

"To any entrepreneur: if you want to do it, do it now. If you don't, you're going to regret it." — Catherine Cook, Co-founder, MeetMe

"People ask me all the time, 'How can I become a successful entrepreneur?' And I have to be honest: It's one of my least favorite questions, because if you're waiting for someone else's advice to become an entrepreneur, chances are you're not one." — Michael Dell, Chairman & CEO, Dell

"Part of the challenge of being an entrepreneur, if you're going for a really huge opportunity, is trying to find problems that aren't quite on the radar yet and try to solve those." — Sean Parker, Board Member, Spotify

Social Entrepreneur

In 2003, the U.N. Secretary General Kofi Annan called for Silicon Valley's moguls to look outward and to "bring more of its remarkable dynamism and innovation to the developing world." Annan challenged Silicon Valley's business community to become **social entrepreneurs**, activists that brandish the methodologies of *entrepreneurship* against societal or environmental problems. While business *entrepreneurs* might construct completely new industries, social entrepreneurs might vastly improve how people interact with the world around them.

A social entrepreneur may start a for-profit company with a social mission or a nonprofit organization that uses cutting-edge business techniques and approaches. Social entrepreneurs ideally have a sense of social purpose embedded in their *business model*, allowing for **shared value initiatives** that provide both economic and social benefit. Other social entrepreneurs may apply some of the firm's profits or revenues to charity or (as required for certified **B-corporation** status) agree to certain "best practices" in dealing with suppliers, employees, or the environment, even if unrelated to the core *business model*. The **benefit corporation** is an alternative organizational structure that shields social entrepreneurs by limiting their fiduciary responsibility to maximize shareholder value at all costs.

Social entrepreneurs and their organizations may themselves benefit from **impact investing**, which places capital in organizations that address social or environmental issues with the dual intentions of 1) advancing the organization's mission in a measurable way and 2) generating a financial return—with varying amounts of emphasis on each. The **double bottom line** represents an effort to operationalize both intentions. It is sometimes extended to a **triple bottom line**, comprising social, environmental, and financial effects. There is debate over whether or not such concerns reduce financial returns; on the assumption they do such investments are considered **concessionary**.

Fixing the world has become trendy, so conscientious folks should be wary of companies' tendency to **greenwash** (adapted from whitewash) their activities, making them appear more socially beneficial than is actually the case.

Example sentences:

I am an admirer of John Wood, the social entrepreneur who founded the non-profit Room to Read.

He objects to the term 'social entrepreneur' on the grounds that every business must satisfy the needs of its customers, who make up society.

She's seeking an opportunity for impact investment that tackles global warming.

Quotes:

"Social entrepreneurs identify resources where people only see problems. They view the villagers as the solution, not the passive beneficiary. They begin with the assumption of competence and unleash resources in the communities they're serving." — David Bornstein, Author, *How to Change the World*

"Social entrepreneurs are not content just to give a fish or teach how to fish. They will not rest until they have revolutionized the fishing industry." — Bill Drayton, CEO, Ashoka

"Lately there is a lot of buzz in Silicon Valley about social impact investing. Startup executives and venture capitalists with an earnest gleam in their eyes increasingly talk about using hi-tech to make the world a better place for everyone—rather than just vying for the multimillion-dollar exit." — Oded Ben-Dov, Co-founder & CEO, Sesame Enable

Unicorn

VCs bet their *limited partners'* money on companies—most of which they know will fail—in the hope that one will succeed so wildly that it will pay for all the others and still make them a killing. But they have no idea which one will be that rare **unicorn**.

Everybody is looking for unicorns, but nobody knows what they look like (until the horn grows in). It may be possible to identify companies that will do well, but it's impossible to predict those, and only those, that will be unicorns, in part because the formula for success is constantly changing. Investor Peter Thiel has noted that although most *disruptive* ideas at first sound crazy (think AirBnB), it is just as true that most ideas that sound crazy really are. Every *startup* wants to be a unicorn, but the challenge is how to get just the right combination of innovative product idea, implementation, timing, chemistry among *co-founders*, and, just maybe, a little magic...

Since Cowboy Ventures Founder Aileen Lee popularized the term "unicorn" in a November 2013 blog post, the focus of the term has shifted to indicate a *startup* whose *valuation* exceeds $1 billion. But as promising companies now wait longer before doing *IPOs*, allowing eager investors time to pour in more money, the number of private companies reaching the magic $1 billion dollar *valuation* mark is growing. And indeed some companies now purposefully aim for that figure, viewing it as a status symbol. Inflated *values* have raised the bar to **decacorn** status of $10 billion. In her post, Lee noted that in contrast to Silicon Valley lore, twenty-something *co-founders* are rare among unicorns, as are significant *pivots*.

As concerns about a tech bubble intensify, unicorns are beginning to attract negative attention as examples of firms that have raised more money than is justified by their actual business potential. Some predict that many will fail and end up as **unicorpses**.

Example sentences:

A few unicorns produce the majority of the returns in the venture capital business.

The lucky investor bragged about the unicorn in her portfolio.

The focus on unicorns is viewed by some as a sign that another tech bubble is in the making.

Quotes:

"Judging by the volume of recent news coverage, one might think you can't walk around Silicon Valley anymore without tripping over a unicorn." — Peter Barris, Managing General Partner, New Enterprise Associates

"VCs often put money into late stage unicorns so they can point to their investing prowess when the company has a successful exit." — John Backus, Co-founder & Managing Partner, New Atlantic Ventures

"From some, there's even concern now that pursuit of 'unicornhood' is both annoying and may have somehow changed the nature of tech valuations." — Aileen Lee, Founder, Cowboy Ventures

"Having a $1 billion valuation can be a real problem ... Being a unicorn is really an albatross." — John Doerr, Partner, Kleiner Perkins Caufield & Byers

"Moral hazard and exuberance to make unicorns leads to unicorpses." — Derek Pilling, Managing Partner, Tahosa Capital

"A ridiculous amount of unicorns have a $1 billion valuation. Why is that? Because it is a purpose in itself. You know that the owners of the company have done terms—liquidation preferences maybe 2x, 3x, but aggressive—to get to that $1 billion." — Pieter van der Does, Co-founder & CEO, Adyen

INNOVATION

Disruption

The dream of every Silicon Valley *startup* is to **disrupt** an industry—to produce an innovation so different from what came before that it is a **game-changer** that upends the status quo and becomes **the next big thing**. Such innovations create **disruption** as those relying on traditional business models are left at a competitive disadvantage. The idea of "disrupting the X industry" is also often expressed in shorthand as "disrupt X." Disruption often involves seeing what others don't; sometimes it involves seeing the world in a whole new way. That is referred to as a **paradigm shift**. When expressing a desire to engage in disruptive innovation, the phrase **break shit** may also be used. This is the opposite of "if it's not broken, don't fix it" and reflects a desire to upend established ways of doing things. The constant disruption that occurs in Silicon Valley leads to a cycle of **creative destruction**, in which new products and new companies are constantly emerging while old ones fade away.

The term **disruptive technology** was introduced by Joseph Bower and Clayton Christensen in a 1995 article titled "Disruptive Technologies: Catching the Wave" and then further explored by Christensen in his book *The Innovator's Dilemma*. Christensen later changed his term to **disruptive innovation** to capture the idea that the *business model* that the technology enables is what creates the disruptive impact. Christensen's work distinguished between sustaining (quantitative) innovations and disruptive (qualitative) ones and considered how upstarts can drive more established companies out of business using simpler, disruptive solutions that focus on product attributes ignored by the market leaders. Because the disruptive solution tends to have lower margins, market leaders are unlikely to take it up.

While the word "disrupt" creates a sparkle in the eye of every *entrepreneur*, it is more likely to instill fear in a corporate executive. Such executives are most likely to avoid this fate by practicing **continuous innovation**, i.e., focusing on constantly improving their offerings rather than on milking cash cows.

Example sentences:

He thinks that the next big thing will be custom 3D-printing of plastics.

Our startup is looking to disrupt dry cleaning.

Pied Piper's compression technology is sure to be a game-changer.

Quotes:

"I have a feeling that a lot of these 'on demand' companies aren't going to be as game-changing as we think—and will come back down to earth with valuations that look more like temp agencies than the next big thing." — Charlie O'Donnell, Partner, Brooklyn Bridge Ventures

"... when your mission is based around creating customer value, around creating great products, cannibalization and disruption aren't 'bad things' to be avoided. They're things you actually strive for—because they let you improve the outcome for your customer." — James Allworth, Director of Strategy, Medallia

"These days, a congratulatory use of the phrase 'break shit' seems to reflect the Silicon Valley ethos that there are no incremental improvements or careful course corrections. There is only revolution." — Katy Waldman, Assistant Editor, *Slate*

"Disrupt or be disrupted. The consultants and business book writers have proclaimed that as the chronic condition of the age, and everybody is clambering to be classed among the disruptors rather than the disruptees." — Geoff Nunberg, Professor, School of Information, University of California at Berkeley

X For Y

X for Y is an expression of an analogy in which an *entrepreneur's* product or service is said to have a similar *business model* to a well-known, established company (X), but *targeting* a different *market segment* or *use case* (Y). For example, "Airbnb for boats" describes a *startup* that applies a *sharing economy business model* to boats, rather than to homes and apartments. On the theory that "there is nothing new under the sun," or at least nothing easy, the "X for Y" approach is a natural one in adapting a successful formula to a new situation.

As the basis of a *pitch*, "X for Y" is appealing because it is simple and succinct, efficiently describing a *business model* to a potential investor in seconds. Comparing the *startup* to a known entity helps investors quickly get the idea. And by referencing a proven approach, it makes success seem more likely. As a form of **high concept pitch**, "X for Y" distills a *startup*'s vision into a single sentence.

There are also downsides to the "X for Y" approach. Oversimplifying a product or service's definition can misrepresent it, and all analogies are imperfect—both *founders* and investors can be blinded to significant differences between the two situations. If a product is truly unique, that can be lost in an "X for Y" analogy. Moreover, the very attempt to define a *startup* in this way is likely to lead to ideas not nearly as ground-breaking as the original. Another drawback is that "X for Y" has become over-used and, therefore, trite. A parody site, itsthisforthat.com, randomly generates *pitches* like "collaborative filter for nightclub lines" and "analytics *platform* for Erlang enthusiasts." A pitch that relies too much on an X for Y analogy risks making a startup look superficial and in need of more precise *positioning*.

Example sentences:

As the new Instagram for video, my business model will surely be extremely profitable.

My startup is like Pandora for Internet cat videos.

I'm getting bored of hearing all these "X for Y" pitches.

Quotes:

"Tech startups that matter create categories rather than refine one. Dropbox, Google, Facebook, [AngelList], Zillow, Parse, Heroku, and Rackspace couldn't be described as "X for Y" businesses." — Michael Girdley, Founder & CEO, Codeup

"One of the most frustrating parts of my early investor pitches for LabDoor was my inability to generate an appropriate 'X for Y' comparison. The easiest way to help investors 'pattern recognize' and understand the concept and business model of a startup is to connect it to past successes." — Neil Thanedar, Founder & CEO, LabDoor

"I am tired of hearing 'Uber for X', 'Airbnb for Y' or 'eBay for Z' analogies. Focus on what problem your business solves for its customers." — Hiten Shah, Co-founder, KISSmetrics

"Repeat after me: you are not the Airbnb of industry x, y or even z." — Matt Murphy, General Partner, Kleiner Perkins Caufield & Byers

"A high concept pitch distills a startup's vision into a single sentence. It's the perfect tool for fans and investors who are spreading the word about your company." — Babak Nivi, Founder, AngelList

"A 'We're X for Y' type pitch is training wheels for your product marketing. Good when you're figuring it out, bad if you can't get past it." — Des Traynor, Co-founder, Intercom

Stealth Mode

Stealth mode, a term borrowed from the military, refers to a period when *startups* keep quiet about their plans. Stealth mode is primarily meant to prevent a competitor, especially one with greater resources, from getting wind of the idea and developing it first. It is particularly relevant before *IP* is filed.

Variations exist on the level of stealth enforced; some companies develop their product under complete cover and even go so far as to start with a company name different than the intended company name (which could be a tip-off to what they're creating). Companies in stealth mode will require an *NDA* before sharing anything of substance about their activities.

Numerous early-stage companies now say that they are in stealth mode regardless of whether they actually are or need to be. Some may feel that the super-secrecy imparts an aura of mystery and great expectations, almost a form of PR in and of itself to drive greater interest in the company.

There are also disadvantages to stealth mode. A certain amount of open disclosure is needed to win over co-*founders*, employees, and business partners, not to mention investors, and to generate "buzz." So clamming up is not always the best approach.

A similar term is **skunk works**. Originally the name of a Lockheed Martin project that was kept under wraps, it is now used more generally to refer to projects within larger companies that are granted both secrecy and autonomy. But skunk works projects were isolated as much for the benefit of the rest of the company as for their own—lest the chaos of *disruptive innovation* infect highly regulated process innovation.

Example sentences:

When I asked for a demo he told me they were still in stealth mode.

I have no idea what they're building—they're in stealth mode.

I had to sign an NDA because they're in stealth mode on that project.

Quotes:

"There are varying degrees of stealth, ranging from companies that won't tell anyone what they are up to, to companies ... that don't have a web site and haven't made any announcement of their business intentions or funding but aren't hiding what they are doing in daily industry conversations, etc." — Seth Levine, Managing Director, Foundry Group

"Stealth mode implicitly suggests a heightened level of pretension. The underlying message is, 'What we are doing is so mind-blowing, so unique, so incredible, I can't tell you about it.' Really? I doubt it." — John Greathouse, Partner, Rincon Venture Partners

"Working in extreme secrecy, or, to use the argot of the moment, operating in 'stealth mode' is an increasingly standard part of a startup's journey from idea-glimmer to full-fledged company ... Increasingly, stealth mode is used not just to protect intellectual property, but also—and more often solely— to build buzz in the media and amongst consumers." — Christine Lagorio, Senior Writer, *Inc.*

"With the vantage point of the 21st century, we can now see that a successful skunk works—separated from its corporate parent, with its own culture, in control of its own R&D and distribution channel—*looked much like a startup.*" — Steve Blank, Author, *The Startup Owner's Manual*

Crowdsourcing

A sponsor company **crowdsources** services, ideas, or *content* by soliciting contributions from a large number of people (a **crowd**) rather than from employees in a chain of command or from organized suppliers. It is an alternative way to generate input on, or actions that support, a company's business activities. Crowdsourced *content* that is intended to persist online is known as **user-generated content**.

First coined in 2005, the word "crowdsource" blends together the words "crowd" and "outsource." Its current usage in Silicon Valley refers mostly to crowdsourcing done online.

Opening an organization to input from the crowd unlocks creativity, skills, experience, and perspectives beyond the limits of the internal team. It can generate invaluable feedback from potential users or help solve problems. Crowdsourcing can also involve the deployment of a crowd of freelancers to take on small tasks as independent contractors, such as tagging photos, that are otherwise inefficient to engage in.

Crowd participants may be volunteers or paid. Both sides of the crowdsourcing construct always benefit in one way or another, whether through cash payment or less tangible means such as simple recognition. While crowds can sometimes be motivated to participate through *gamification,* paid crowdsourcing of services is becoming widespread, known (somewhat derisively) as the **gig economy** and typified by sites such as UpWork (contracting professional work) and TaskRabbit (contracting errands and miscellaneous tasks).

More general crowdsourced *content* can be aggregated in a **wiki**, a community-maintained store of knowledge, of which Wikipedia is by far the largest instance. The chaos of the community is often managed via *version control* and other mechanisms.

A related concept to crowdsourcing is **open innovation**, which takes crowd involvement a step further by involving outsiders more deeply in the firm's creative processes through greater information flow into and out of the organization.

Example sentences:

They plan to crowdsource all the labor for their new project.

She didn't think of herself as a provider of crowdsourced content ... until being reminded of her reviews on Internet shopping sites.

These gig economy jobs let me work when I want, but the pay isn't always so great!

Quotes:

"The most viable approach for startups is crowdsourcing the data. This boils down to designing a service that provides the right incentives for users to give data back to the system to make it better." — Chris Dixon, General Partner, Andreessen Horowitz

"With nearly 300 million passenger vehicles in the states, it's economically and environmentally irresponsible NOT to crowdsource package delivery." — Gerrit Hall, CEO, Sand Hill Exchange

"Crowdsourcing is the ultimate disruptor of distribution because in a most Zen-like fashion, the content is controlled by everyone and no one at the same time." — Jay Samit, Serial Entrepreneur and Author, *Disrupt You!*

"As I've conducted my interviews with crowdsourcing entrepreneurs and experts, it's constantly hit me that your ability to do something big and bold is really a function of the size and quality of your crowd." — Peter Diamandis, Chairman & CEO, X PRIZE Foundation

NDA

When a firm needs to share ideas that are likely a tremendous, if not its most significant, asset, a **non-disclosure agreement**, or NDA (sometimes referred to as a **confidentiality agreement**) can help protect that information. Such agreements define the relevant information, the purpose for which it is expected to be used, and any limitations on the confidentiality restrictions. NDAs may be mutual (covering both parties' information) or one-directional.

Whether or not signing NDAs is appropriate is one of the more polarizing issues in the Valley. Which is the greater impediment to trust, requesting an NDA or refusing to sign one? Are they even enforceable? Companies will often ask for an NDA to be signed before entering discussions likely to entail sharing detailed information about their products or businesses. The NDA is now so commonplace in *startup* culture that you will often hear in conversations: "Happy to sign an NDA" when two parties are coming together for the first time to consider a business relationship. Many Silicon Valley companies now require that all visitors to their offices sign an NDA as a condition for entry to the premises. On the other hand, many *venture capitalists* and other investors refuse to sign NDAs, on the grounds that they review many similar ideas and don't want to risk legal liability if they fund a different one.

Perhaps the greatest legal significance of the NDA is its potential use in enforcement of *IP* rights. Discussion of one's ideas without the precaution of a signed NDA could be considered a public disclosure, which could preclude obtaining a *patent*. Furthermore, an *NDA* is the best way to ensure that expectations regarding sharing of information are well understood. For these reasons, even *VCs* may advise *startups* to require NDAs from people other than themselves.

Example sentences:

I was put off when he expected me to sign an NDA at our first meeting.

Before the meeting began, the parties passed around the NDA.

Let's sign an NDA before going any deeper.

Quotes:

"Non-disclosure agreements (NDA) have become so commonplace that they are now referred to as the 'Silicon Valley Handshake.'" — Robert Bleicher, Director, CarrMcClellan

"In some circles, any conversation beyond pleasantries requires an NDA." — Eric Goldman, Professor of Law, School of Law, Santa Clara University

"I will not sign an NDA and prefer passing on the deal." — Shlomo Kramer, Founder & CEO, Cato Networks

"Not a single VC or investor I know will ever sign an NDA. Why? They see hundreds of ideas every month and have so many discussions with several people. There is no way that they can [ever] realistically know if they are protecting confidentiality at the level of an idea." — G. Venkat, Venture Partner, Naya Ventures

"NDAs are a special sort of contract. By their very existence, they implicitly announce that a handshake is not good enough. They basically say, 'I don't trust you.' This matters because distrust is the silent killer of innovation. When parties ask for NDAs too early, it can stifle relationships before they are born. Or they can slow down relationships for extra days, weeks, even months. They can add suspicion and sow the seeds of disharmony later." — Victor Hwang, CEO, Liquidity

IP

Intellectual Property, or simply **IP**, describes creations of the mind. IP can be registered under law in any one of the following three methods: copyright, trademark or *patent*. IP also includes **trade secrets**, which are not registered but are protected if stolen in violation of an *NDA*. Trade secrets might include assets such as customer lists, or a formula, practice, process, or method, that is not generally known by others and that a business uses to obtain an economic advantage.

A **copyright** protects creative works in a tangible form. Books, music, and other creative works are covered under copyright. Unauthorized replication of the copyrighted work is prohibited. Fair use of copyrighted material, however, is acceptable, and the "border cases" can be controversial.

In contrast, a **trademark** protects a company's markings (i.e., slogans, sounds, colors, logos) that distinguish it and its products from competitors. The standard is whether a customer would be confused about the source of merchandise or a service.

Patents, on the other hand, protect inventions that are useful, novel, and non-obvious.

For *startups*, IP is a form of **barrier to entry**, inhibiting competitors that attempt to enter the firm's market or recreate its products or services. Getting the IP rights in place is one of the important steps that a firm can take toward strengthening its competitive position and also increasing its potential *valuation*. An IP strategy should evaluate all the firm's IP assets and how they can be protected over the course of their useful life. It should also consider the IP assets of competitors, and how they can be countered.

Example sentences:

A high priority for a new startup is to lock down its IP.

Investors will be interested in the strength of a startup's IP portfolio.

What's your IP strategy?

Quotes:

"Intellectual property gives you rights to stop others from using your creativity." — Steve Blank, Author, *The Startup Owner's Manual*

"If your startup starts to scale quickly, a strong IP portfolio will be vitally important to your ability to play the long game." — Kelly Fitzsimmons, Co-founder, Hypervoice Consortium

"Company founders should talk about IP early and often. They should teach company employees about the importance of IP and how it works, or better yet, they should ask their IP attorney to teach them." — Scott Smith, Partner, Dorsey & Whitney

"Venture capitalists, angel investors and start-up lawyers these days tend to be obsessed with 'intellectual property,' or IP. And for good reason: In the information economy, the core assets of a new venture are likely to be talented people, the IP they create, and little else." — Antone Johnson, Founding Principal, Bottom Line Law Group

"Not too long ago, defensible IP was one of the top things venture capitalists wanted to see in a startup. But the success of several high-profile tech startups, such as Twitter and Facebook, that are relatively weak on patentable intellectual property, has caused many to rethink that assumption." — Kelly Fitzsimmons, Co-founder, Hypervoice Consortium

Patent

Patents are the part of an *IP* portfolio that protects inventions, as defined in a *patent* application through a set of **claims**. Patents protect inventions that are useful, novel, and not obvious. Utility patents protect the functional characteristics of inventions, while design patents protect ornamental characteristics of functional items. Functional characteristics of inventions may be expressed as a method (process), a composition of matter, a machine, or an article of manufacture.

Patents are a social contract by which the inventor is granted exclusivity in exchange for explaining the invention in sufficient detail for one to construct it. Patents prohibit others from making or using the invention without authorization for a set period of time. A patent does not, however, imply the owner's right to make or use the invention, i.e., **freedom to operate**, as the invention may **infringe** on other patents.

Patents are often surrounded by controversy and patent law (both statutory and case law) changes frequently. Patents protecting business methods are currently frowned upon, and the scope of software patents is in flux. **Patent trolls**, or NPEs (**non-practicing entities**), attempt to enforce their patent rights against accused infringers although they themselves do not manufacture products or supply services using those patents. They receive the disdain of large corporations that, like a cartel, prefer to maintain their collective position in an uneasy balance of power, threatening each other with lawsuits. NPEs have been associated with abusive practices such as threatening small businesses with expensive lawsuits on the basis of weak patents, but may represent a small independent inventor's best route to *monetizing* his or her inventions.

Patents can be expensive and time-consuming to obtain, which adds to their *value* and strategic importance. But litigating patents is even more difficult and unlikely to happen until a lot is at stake.

Example sentences:

After all of the back-and-forth with the patent office, he was overjoyed when his patent application was accepted.

The investor thought that the venture's patent expenses were premature, as the value of the invention had not been demonstrated.

She was unable to extend her product in the manner she intended because another firm had already applied for that patent.

Quotes:

"On the plus side, some patents (a very small percentage) become very valuable some time in the future. They are either valuable for defense against other patent suits or they can be used offensively against competitors or they can be monetized in some way. On the minus side, patents take time and money to acquire." — John Friend, Principal, Softworks Consulting

"Every piece of software written today is likely going to infringe on someone else's patent." — Miguel de Icaza, CTO, Xamarin

"I think you would find almost anyone who stands up for their patent rights has been called a patent troll." — Nathan Myhrvoid, Co-founder, Intellectual Ventures

"The under-funded and over-extended United States Patent and Trademark Office does not have the resources to adequately evaluate the burgeoning number of applications, and too many low-quality patents are being issued as a result." — Viet D. Dinh, Founding Partner, Bancroft, PLLC

"In my career as a patent examiner, many of the patents that moved forward succeeded on a technicality, not because they showcased groundbreaking innovation." — G. Nagesh Rao, Chief Technologist, U.S. Small Business Administration

Fail Fast

Traditionally, failure was only considered as a negative, but Silicon Valley has developed a new way of thinking about it. Because innovation rarely takes the form of a straight line, failures are inevitable on the way to success. From this perspective, in Silicon Valley failure is commonly worn as a badge of honor, not shame, among *entrepreneurs*. The key is to effectively learn from the failures during the course of creating, executing, refining, *iterating*, or *pivoting*.

It is natural that failure be flaunted like a diploma, because failure is a form of education. We learn from failure, because it makes us stop and reconsider our actions and thought processes. **Fail forward** is a commonly-used Silicon Valley expression that reflects this ethos. To fail forward is to learn from what went wrong and view every event—no matter how negative—as feedback to be mined for wisdom.

It stands to follow that the more often we can fail, the more accelerated the education. Of course, one doesn't fail just for the sake of failing. But if failure is received objectively, one can bounce back quickly and resume one's education—the trial and error process that may ultimately yield success. *Design thinking* and *Agile development methodologies* rely on this perspective. If something you are doing is not working, it's important to not just keep doing the same thing, but rather to **fail fast** and nimbly change course.

The idea that failure breeds success is now considered to be part of Silicon Valley culture. Such sentiments are easily expressed but not so easily assumed, either by an organization or an individual. In the corporate case, can one achieve success without incentivizing for it? Perhaps this difficulty is for the best. If one accepts failure too easily, what remains of the drive to succeed? And if one experiences failure too often, might that become the expectation?

Example sentences:

He was a firm believer in the fail fast approach.

Entrepreneurs are often given the advice that they should fail fast.

She spent a day mourning the loss of her startup before failing forward with a new idea.

Quotes:

"Ever tried. Ever failed. No matter. Try again. Fail again. Fail better." — Samuel Beckett, via Richard Branson, CEO, The Virgin Group

"The alternate name we came up with for 500 Startups was 'fail factory,' ... if you're not willing to take the risk of failing ..., you're never going to figure out what the right path is to success." — Dave McClure, Founding Partner, 500 Startups

"Tell that to the person who wrote you $50,000 of their hard earned money and entrusted you to try your best. Fail fast? How does your brother-in-law feel about that?" — Mark Suster, Partner, Upfront Ventures

"Fail fast isn't about the big issues, it's about the little ones. It's an approach to running a company or developing a product that embraces lots of little experiments with the idea that some will work and grow and others will fail and die." — David Brown, Managing Partner, Techstars

"For most entrepreneurs—and let's face it, for most anyone—failure is painful. But if you're an entrepreneur setting out to create something original and sustainable, failure is not just inevitable, it must become a foundation for your success. Think of it as failing forward." — Tim Ogilvie, CEO, Peer Insight

Design Thinking

Thinking like a designer means finding ways to seamlessly and simply meet human needs, while balancing technical feasibility and economic viability. Although **design thinking** has its origins in processes used to design physical products, it can apply to many disciplines. Some of its steps are similar to those of *Lean Startup*, but design thinking is a more collaborative and deliberate process focusing on more expansive problems and thus more concerned with **ideation**. It has been applied, for example, to designing an activity meter and motivational website to fight obesity, a neonatal baby-warmer for use in rural areas, and ways to increase the accessibility of quality higher education. It is used both in traditional corporate settings and in the developing world.

Design thinking begins with an open mind, without preconceptions or constraints. It initially involves research, first academic research of the system of interest and then direct observation of its operation, with empathy for those involved. Through a process of synthesis involving knowledge representation tools, these disparate learnings coalesce to form a system model. Only with the benefit of that model and understanding is a specific problem defined and the floor opened to brainstorming solutions—the more, the better. Ideas are recorded on post-it notes so that they can easily be rearranged and combined. The most promising ideas are continually nurtured and expanded on through a process of refinement. Eventually, the group constructs one or more tangible *prototypes* of the most compelling solutions, which are introduced into the system. Based on feedback, any of the preceding steps are repeated as necessary.

While design thinking has had many success stories, its attempts to boil creativity down to a formulaic series of steps (different depending on who you ask) may discount the complex and messy interactions that lead to good design, while downplaying the importance of the talented facilitator in the room.

Example sentences

The charity is applying design thinking to the challenges faced in the developing world.

Weeks after the design thinking session, they were still finding post-it notes.

The team got along much better after doing a design thinking exercise together.

Quotes:

"We kept looking for new ways to instill design thinking. To help things along, we even tried changing the layout of our office spaces. We reduced the number of cubes and added more areas for collaboration and impromptu work." — Brad Smith, CEO, Intuit

"Design thinking attempts to inspire the essential element of creativity, the ability to take an abstract idea and create something with it." — Reuven Cohen, Chief Technology Advocate, Citrix

"For all the gushing success stories that we and others wrote, most were often focused on one small project executed at the periphery of a multinational organization. When we stopped and looked, it seemed like executives had issues rolling out design thinking more widely throughout the firm." — Helen Walters, Editorial Director, TED

"From the beginning, the process of Design Thinking was a scaffolding for the real deliverable: creativity. But in order to appeal to the business culture of process, it was denuded of the mess, the conflict, failure, emotions, and looping circularity that is part and parcel of the creative process. In a few companies, CEOs and managers accepted that mess along with the process and real innovation took place. In most others, it did not." — Tim Brown, CEO, IDEO

Scalability

To **scale**, in its simplest form, means to grow from some current state to a much larger one. A key question *VCs* will use as a filter to evaluate any *startup* concept is "Will it scale?"

The ability to scale requires two things: a practically limitless *total addressable market* and diminishing marginal costs. The market can grow by providing more services to existing users, but ultimately it will be necessary to serve a broad array of users. Diminishing marginal costs allow a business to grow quickly because less work is needed to obtain (*customer acquisition cost*) and serve each additional customer.

Consider a **brick and mortar** business, i.e., one operating out of a physical location, like a specialty bookstore. Since it is constrained by geography and by the number of people that can physically visit the store, sales will inevitably plateau. Attempting to increase sales by taking on new titles requires more shelf space, which increases costs, as does opening additional stores in new locations. Now consider the introduction of an Internet site where users can buy and sell books among each other. The market is almost limitless and shelf space and inventory are unnecessary. The business has now become **scalable**.

Ideally, any business wants to keep costs at a minimum and expand growth as quickly as possible. In a *startup* company, the objective, by definition, is extremely rapid growth, making scalable solutions key to achieving success. But scaling too early can be a curse. The only thing more important to a *startup* than scaling is learning; scaling without an infrastructure to service and upgrade customers risks slowing down product enhancement and thus the learning process. Scaling too rapidly can also lead to deficiencies in product quality and customer service that alienate customers and scar the *startup's* reputation.

Example sentences:

They hadn't optimized their business model for scalability and didn't anticipate the costs of growth.

Most startup founders are eager to scale their businesses.

The startup was killed by scaling before having a proven business model.

Quotes:

"Scaling refers to the period in a startup's life when management and board [feel] like they can systematically accelerate growth with confidence that the resources they put in will yield great and measurable results." — Fred Destin, General Partner, Accel

"Startups need 2-3 times longer to validate their market than most founders expect. This under-estimation creates the pressure to scale prematurely." — Bjoern Lasse Herrmann, Author, *Startup Genome*

"To grow rapidly, you need to make something you can sell to a big market. That's the difference between Google and a barbershop. A barbershop doesn't scale." — Paul Graham, Co-founder, Y Combinator

"It has been said that the truest test of scaling is 'replacing all components of a car while driving it at 100 mph.' If the car is still intact, you've got a scalable model." — Shane Barker, VP, Digital Marketing, Kamere

"Scaling is actually a problem of less ... There are lots of things that used to work that don't work anymore, so you have to get rid of them. There are probably a bunch of things you've always done that slowed you down without you realizing it." — Bob Sutton, Professor of Management Science & Engineering, Stanford University

Hackathon

Hackathon, a portmanteau of *hack* and "marathon," describes a competitive event in which teams of developers (potentially also graphic designers, interface designers, and project managers) come together to build software. While some hackathons are one-day events, many, as suggested by "marathon," take place over several days.

A hackathon may be focused around a specific topic, e.g., mobile apps, *connected car* technologies, or a specific operating system. Some hackathons are conducted as contests, with teams formed at the beginning, and the winner determined by a panel of investors to which they ultimately *pitch* and *demo* their *prototype*. Other hackathons are sponsored by organizations, especially non-profits, to gather technological solutions to problems that they wish to address. Hackathons are often sponsored by companies that have released a *platform/API,* with the intention of encouraging developers to build applications around it. A hackathon might be open to the public or only to a company's employees.

The beauty of the hackathon is the interplay of the collaborative and competitive aspects; many minds and sets of eyes can geometrically increase the potential of teams in a time-constrained setting.

Given the marathon nature of the hackathon, one should not be shocked to find the venue littered with the standard fare of energy drinks, pizza, and granola bars, and fallen *hackers* sleeping at random on the floor.

Example sentences:

My company is putting on an internal one-day hackathon.

They were excited to attend the hackathon sponsored by five of the largest tech companies.

The hackathon was devoted to apps that help veterans.

Quotes:

"My love of hackathons, 24–48 hour hacking marathons, started at my first Startup Weekend in Pittsburgh four years ago. The idea of bringing together ambitious entrepreneurs, developers and designers to work on an idea that tickled the back of your brain was compelling." — Brittany Martin, Devops/ Software Engineer, Northwest Independent Ruby Development

"There's a lot to be said for hackathons: They give the technology community great social opportunities and reward them with money and fame for their solutions, and companies get free access to a community of diligent experts they otherwise wouldn't know how to reach." — Jake Porway, Founder & Executive Director, DataKind

"Anyone can attend a hackathon with zero prior experience, and, by the end of the weekend, have the newfound ability to create." — Dave Fontenot, Founder, HackMatch

"Hackathons are a great place to get your hands dirty ... Even as a first timer working with three people I just met, I learned how to develop an idea, design a solution, and execute a product." — Sagar Rambhia, Innovation Fellow, University Hospitals of Cleveland

"Companies like Salesforce have hijacked hackathons to get free projects, apps, and ideas (and in this instance, code) out of developers in exchange for some cold pizza, without any of the spirit of what hackathons were originally supposed to be about." — Alicia Liu, Senior Software Engineer, Lift Worldwide

Dogfooding

In *startup* culture, to "**eat your own dog food**" means using your own product or service internally as a way to validate its quality and capabilities.

In 1981, Microsoft manager Paul Maritz titled an office email "Eating our own dog food," by which he challenged the recipients to increase internal usage of the company's product. From there, use of the term spread through the company like wildfire and was eventually taken up throughout Silicon Valley. The idea is that if you expect your customers to use your products and services, you should expect no less from your own employees. **Dogfooding** as a verb also has come to mean the same thing.

Testing one's own products in real life scenarios can't be overrated. *Agile development methodologies* emphasize close interaction with users, and there is no closer interaction than that among your own employees. By dogfooding before *launch* to customers, management can gather information from their employees' experience about what features need improvement and what changes would be helpful. But having your product in your own workflow can provide more than data. It opens you up to the same frustrations as your customers, giving a more visceral and intuitive understanding of the *user experience*. Employees may even get ideas for other *use cases* they hadn't contemplated.

Moreover, if a firm believes that the principles on which its product is based are valid, it must also believe that using that product will provide it with real *value* and competitive advantage. Furthermore, the assurance provided to potential customers by the fact that a firm is willing to entrust its own well-being to its product can be invaluable.

Example sentences:

They were dogfooding that concept for a long time before release.

The best advice the VC gave me was to "eat my own dog food."

They'd have caught that problem if they were dogfooding.

Quotes:

"Dogfooding in our company creates a nice virtuous cycle (improving the product improves the company's efficiency at improving the product ...). It also means that when we're prioritizing features, we're motivated directly by our own experience with the product." — Justin Rosenstein, Co-founder, Asana

"To start-ups who tell me that they dogfood their product all the time, I say that's great. But remember, to actually eat dogfood you have to open a brand new packet, every single day." — Des Traynor, Co-founder, Intercom

"We realized we weren't sure that we did a good job ourselves at being customer-centric. With that in mind, we decided to eat our own dog food and ask the market how we were doing." — Brad Svrluga, Co-founder & General Partner, Primary Venture Partners

"When tech behemoths like Apple and Google need to work the bugs out of their latest miracle creation, they want eyes on it, pronto. And that means everyone from the CEO to the lowliest intern is going to be eating a lot of dogfood." — Nora Caplan-Bricker, Staff Correspondent, *National Journal*

"The commonly touted benefit of dogfooding is the ability to catch bugs because you're using the product outside a structured QA script." — Michael Keoni DeFranco, Founder & CEO, Lua

Beta Test

If a *startup* is following an *Agile methodology*, it will be reviewing ideas and *prototypes* with potential customers from early in the development process. Such **alpha testing** generally occurs with a select group of forgiving users before the product is complete. Alpha users tend to be from no more than a few organizations, perhaps including the company itself. Alpha users may be observed directly and/or interviewed about their experience with the product.

A **beta test** involves a less carefully selected and less forgiving group of users as a final step before the product is **launched** for the general public. It is intended to simulate use by paying customers and uncover any remaining problems. Beta testers may be culled from enthusiasts of the business or technology area who have an underlying interest in the product and may therefore be more willing to put up with occasional problems and offer feedback than average users. The beta test, however, is in an unconstrained setting (generally the web), where users can be observed only by their actions. **Beta users** (participants in a beta test) are intended to be full-fledged users of the product. A company can leverage a beta test to provide publicity for the upcoming launch.

A **pilot** differs from a beta test in that it is scheduled after a customer has decided (at least tentatively) to deploy the product. It therefore usually involves only that organization and is as much for its benefit as for that of the company. The pilot will often use only a portion of the customer's data and run in parallel with its legacy system.

These various levels of user interaction to some extent reflect the natural maturation of an idea into a product. But from the perspective of an innovating organization, they may form a **phase-gate** process by which inferior ideas are filtered out at each stage. In this vein, a **concept and feasibility** study resulting in **proof-of-concept** may be considered the first hurdle.

Example sentences:

Putting your product through a beta test will ensure that the intended audience will relate to the product.

The beta test results were so bad that the company had to terminate it early and make major adjustments to the product.

The users felt much better about deploying the new system after the pilot served as a dry run.

Quotes:

"If you're going to put your product in beta, put your business model in beta with it." — Joe Kraus, Partner, Google Ventures

"Given a large enough beta-tester and co-developer base, almost every problem will be characterized quickly and the fix will be obvious to someone." — Eric S. Raymond, Author, *The Cathedral and the Bazaar*

"The beta program has been successful both in validating some of our product hypotheses and, at least as importantly, providing input about how to allocate our time as we aggressively iterate." — Justin Rosenstein, Co-founder, Asana

"Launching in Beta is a common method to prevent the havoc of an imperfect release, and lately it's been utilized as a promotional technique...The important thing to remember is: Finding great beta testers is key to your startup's success." — Harrison Weber, Executive Editor, *VentureBeat*

"Phase-Gates are reflection points in the project's lifecycle where program management and/or Project sponsors will ask questions to help ensure that sufficient value will be delivered within a reasonable timeframe at a reasonable cost." — Brenda Lynn Petrillo, Global IT Senior Manager & PMO, Honeywell Information Technology

Hype Cycle

VCs and *entrepreneurs* are both, to some extent, herd creatures that chase after whatever is "hot" at the moment, with the hype and excitement building to a frenzy when a promising new technology has been discovered. The hoopla among the early adopters and trend-seekers then dies down as people realize that the new technology is not a panacea, and as their interest moves on to *the next big thing.* The market research and advisory firm Gartner codified these predictable life cycle stages of adoption and diffusion in a graphical representation known as the **Hype Cycle**. Plotting expectations over time, it describes the following five stages:

Technology Trigger. As news of a technology breakthrough spreads, significant publicity and interest are generated. Early adopters investigate and companies that offer the technology proliferate.

Peak of Inflated Expectations. The hype surrounding the concept quickly reaches a frenzied peak. While there are early success stories, there are also failures, especially as use expands beyond early adopters.

Trough of Disillusionment. As users are brought back to reality by the realization that their greatest hopes for the technology may not be met, sentiment takes a plunge and interest wanes. Negative press begins. There is a shakeout of providers, and those that survive need to make improvements in their products. Many technologies and their purveyors stall at this point, failing to **cross the chasm**—the term coined by Geoffrey Moore to describe expansion from early adopters to mainstream markets.

Slope of Enlightenment. A second-generation of products appears, and later a third generation. Methodologies and best practices develop. Adoption grows, and expectations slowly begin to rise again.

Plateau of Productivity. Expectations have leveled out, and high growth mainstream adoption begins.

The concept behind the Hype Cycle curve has creeped into popular language use, with something that epitomizes an overexposed or clichéd trend referred to as "**peak** X."

Example sentences:

Their technology seems to be enjoying a really long hype cycle.

The Mission reached peak hipster years ago.

It's an interesting technology, but I think it's going to have difficulty crossing the chasm to mainstream adoption.

Quotes:

"While there is much optimism around the future potential of self-driving cars, pessimism abounds around the timing of the transition. Pundits believe we are nearing the infamous "Peak of Inflated Expectations" in the Gartner Hype Cycle ... and a long letdown is ahead." — Jake Chapman, Partner, Sazze Partners

"Big Data is showing the first signs of heading for Gartner's Trough of Disillusionment as a spate of voices ... begin to question the hype." — Chris Taylor, Sales Performance Senior Director, TIBCO Software

"There have been numerous criticisms of the hype cycle, one of which is that it is not a cycle, and that all technologies don't really have the same outcome. Another criticism is that the shape of the line has not altered or accelerated in ten years, even though all the evidence suggests that the half-life of new technologies is getting shorter, and the number of competing technologies is increasing." — Martin Zwillig, Founder & CEO, Startup Professionals

"Peak SF: Riding electric motorcycle to pick up Brie and Boudin sourdough baguette." — Roberto Baldwin, Senior Editor, *Engadget*

PRODUCT DEVELOPMENT

Agile Development

Agile development methodologies focus on developing software by *iterating* in short cycles and adapting. They promote respect for and connection among motivated individuals by emphasizing personal responsibility.

Agile was a reaction against **waterfall development**, which takes a more sequential and monolithic approach, first designing, then coding, and finally testing the entire system. And as with navigating a waterfall, backing up is highly discouraged. Such an approach assumes omniscient understanding of a static world, then demands obedience from developers and acquiescence from customers.

Elements of Agile development can be traced back to 1957, although these systems did not become prominent until the 1970s, following the publication of an introductory paper by E.A. Edmonds. In 2001, 17 developers at a summit in Utah introduced the Agile Manifesto, which states: "we have come to value: individuals and interactions over processes and tools; working software over comprehensive documentation; customer collaboration over contract negotiation; responding to change over following a plan." The Agile approach relies on trust; *iterations* provide a chance for that trust to develop.

Scrum is one Agile methodology that emphasizes the dynamics of each *iteration*, specifying various roles, meetings and workflow processes. Another, **Extreme Programming (XP)**, emphasizes efficient and purpose-driven development processes with multiple levels of feedback. A notable one, **test-driven development**, involves writing test cases *before* the code to be tested.

Although the Agile model is not universally accepted, it has become a mainstream development approach in Silicon Valley. While it corrects an imbalance in the other direction, firms should also consider that some solutions may be unlikely to reveal themselves without considerable forethought.

Example sentences:

Agile, which views change as inevitable, fits with his philosophy.

The company he works at is transitioning from waterfall to Agile.

Management had difficulty adjusting to Agile processes.

Quotes:

"The Agile movement is not anti-methodology, in fact many of us want to ... restore a balance. We embrace modeling, but not in order to file some diagram in a dusty corporate repository. We embrace documentation, but not hundreds of pages of never-maintained and rarely-used tomes. We plan, but recognize the limits of planning in a turbulent environment." — Jim Highsmith, Executive Consultant, ThoughtWorks

"We run the company using an Agile development process which, when followed religiously, actually enforces some work-life balance." — Donna Wells, CEO, Mindflash Technologies

"The agile movement is in some ways a bit like a teenager: very self-conscious, checking constantly its appearance in a mirror, accepting few criticisms, only interested in being with its peers, rejecting *en bloc* all wisdom from the past, just because it is from the past, adopting fads and new jargon, at times cocky and arrogant. But I have no doubts that it will mature further, become more open to the outside world, more reflective, and also therefore more effective." — Philippe Kruchten, Professor, University of British Columbia

"What most people believe Agile development is today isn't at all what you need if you're a startup. In fact, trying too hard to get Agile 'right' is a good way to slow down the stuff that should really be happening." — Jeff Patton, Chief Troublemaker, Jeff Patton & Associates

Iteration

Iteration is the process of continually refining and tweaking the features of your product in order to improve it. After introducing a new product, a company will receive and interpret feedback from customers and likely choose to refine the initial concept to incorporate their concerns and experiences. Each cycle is considered an **iteration**. To **iterate** is to perform a sequence of iterations.

An iteration encapsulates a *waterfall development* process, but instead of applying it in a monolithic way, applies it in sequence, so that the project cycles through the various phases, rather than hitting each only once. The structure of an iteration will vary, but it generally proceeds along these lines: define requirements for some ostensible improvement; plan a scope of work; perform the work; present it to end users; and analyze the results. Repeated iterations lead to versions of the product that increasingly meet user needs and wants. What may seem insurmountable when viewed as a single task can sometimes crumble when chipped away at, one iteration at a time.

Iteration is a key principle of *Agile development methodologies* and the *Lean Startup* movement. Iterations, by joining the end of the development process to the beginning, improve both by allowing requirements and design to emerge over time while reducing risk of incompatibilities through frequent product integration. The *Scrum methodology* specifies iterations by fixed blocks of time, and cuts back on the scope of work as needed (**time-boxing**).

Although generally mentioned with respect to bottom-up, forward-searching processes, the notion of iteration might also be applied to top-down ones that begin with a vision of a completed system and work backwards towards achieving it; in reality all projects use a combination of these.

Example sentences:

After several iterations, the product was quickly gaining a user base.

Each iteration made the product a lot better.

Because it covered so much ground in a single iteration, the startup found out late that its new feature was flawed.

Quotes:

"I have always been a bit of a troublemaker at the companies at which I have worked, pushing for rapid iteration, data-driven decision making, and early customer involvement." — Eric Ries, Author, *The Lean Startup*

"The emphasis on the rapid development and iteration of MVP's is to speed up how fast you can learn; from customers, partners, network scale, adoption, etc." — Steve Blank, Author, *The Startup Owner's Manual*

"You must remain in a constant state of discovery, iteration, experimentation, and agility to continue to create value." — Jeremiah Gardner, Author, *The Lean Brand*

"Here's the biggest reason I am in favor of the Iterate Fast philosophy, however: the user knows best. You may believe that ... this set of 13 features is what users want, but you don't really know that until the product is launched." — Ben Parr, Partner, DominateFund

"When I talk to entrepreneurs and they tell me how they've pivoted recently, most of the time they actually mean iterated. Iterate is something you can roll out quickly and casually. Pivoting is a wholesale change to the business and typically takes much longer to execute." — David Cummings, CEO, Atlanta Ventures

Lean Startup

The term **Lean Startup** is inextricably linked with *serial entrepreneur* Eric Ries, who introduced it in a 2008 blog post and published the book by that name in 2011. The Lean Startup methodology brought together *Agile methodologies* and his teacher/mentor Steve Blank's work on **customer development**. The latter emphasized getting extensive feedback on all aspects of the firm's *business model*, including product features, pricing, distribution channels, and customer acquisition strategies. The Lean concept has developed into a full-fledged movement, embraced by thousands in companies of all sizes and spawning its own mini-industry of conferences and consultants.

The Lean Startup methodology incorporates various concepts developed by Blank and/or Ries, including *TAM/SAM*, *MVP*, and the *pivot*, along with the *Agile* notion of *iteration*. Lean Startup can be viewed as applying Agile principles to the firm's entire business model—not taking the customer as the project domain authority, but recognizing that the firm can select from any number of potential customers.

An important contribution addresses the question of how much to invest in projects to prevent problems down the road. **Proportional investment** suggests doing so in proportion to the extent to which the lack of such infrastructure can be pinpointed in the **root cause analysis** of recurring problems and to the *pain* caused by those problems.

The 'lean' in Lean Startup relates not to the amount of funding that a *startup* may have received, but rather to the Japanese practice of lean manufacturing that inspired it. Ultimately, the methodology is about recognizing and responding iteratively to the real needs of customers in order to avoid misdirecting resources. This is embodied in the core slogan of the movement: **Learn-Measure-Build** (as adapted by *Agile* pioneer Kent Beck from Build-Measure-Learn). But as with *Agile methodologies* more generally, Lean Startup's incrementalism may be limited in its applicability—truly revolutionary products may require leaps of faith that the approach cannot quite bridge.

Example sentences:

After taking a six-week course on the Lean Startup method, she felt herself qualified to criticize experienced entrepreneurs.

The Lean Startup approach helped them get the product right.

They're even teaching Lean Startup principles at Harvard Business School.

Quotes:

"The Lean Startup method teaches you how to drive a startup—how to steer, when to turn, and when to persevere—and grow a business with maximum acceleration." — Eric Ries, Author, *The Lean Startup*

"Lean start-ups use a 'get out of the building' approach called customer development to test their hypotheses." — Steve Blank, Author, *The Startup Owner's Manual*

"The Lean Startup approach is not about asking people what they want. It's about understanding the customer, their needs and their pain points. It's about validating that there is a solution and a market before you invest too much money, effort & time into development." — Adrian Howard, Generalising Specialist, Quietstars

"In order to be a Lean Startup you need to change the way decisions are made" — Scott Cook, Founder & Chairman of the Executive Committee, Intuit

"I am personally skeptical of all the Lean Startup methodology. I think the really great companies did something that was sort of a quantum improvement that really differentiated them." — Peter Thiel, Managing Partner, Founders Fund

Prototype

A **prototype** is a simplified version of a product that is intended to convey the **look and feel**, i.e., design elements including the layout and basic workflow, along with varying amounts of functionality, in order to make the concept more concrete with potential investors and validate it with potential customers. At one extreme, a prototype may be a functioning system lacking aesthetic elements or account management features. At the other, it may be a **wireframe**, or **mock-up**, indicating only what each screen looks like and how control flows from one to another. The underlying principle is related to that of the *MVP*, i.e., that one should implement only enough to learn what steps to take next, but the prototype may fall short of the viability criterion. Some prototypes may be intended to be discarded once the lesson has been learned, while others form the basis of the ultimate product. A prototype or mock-up may be presented as a **demo**, short for "demonstration."

As a development tool, mock-ups are extremely important, especially in the early stages of construction. They are an efficient way of validating many hypotheses regarding user behavior and reactions. Functioning much the same way as blueprints, wireframes give developers the ability to experiment with different visual arrangements in order to find a design that visually prioritizes important information and functions and helps assure that the overall goals of a particular page are met. Various software packages allow easy creation of wireframes.

Prototypes generally place emphasis on core functionality rather than appearance. While they can offer a broad idea of how a finished web page will appear, they usually do not focus on creative details such as type treatment and color schemes, nor do they typically use the final text and artwork. Prototypes are a critical tool in *design thinking*.

Example sentences:

We're putting a prototype of our software in front of some test users to see if it really does improve the way the game works.

A good wireframe is like a path through the woods.

This prototype manifests several flaws from the original design.

Quotes:

"I love taking an idea ... to a prototype and then to a product that millions of people use." — Susan Wojcicki, SVP, YouTube

"Once you understand business models you can then start prototyping business models just like you prototype products." — Alexander Osterwalder, Co-founder, Strategyzer

"If you are truly innovating, you don't have a prototype you can refer to." — Jonathan Ive, CDO, Apple

"Standards for prototypes have gone up a lot in recent years due to easy and cheap 3D printing, the low cost of building a website and electronics prototyping with development boards. So in most cases a crude mockup or basic proof of principal model is not going to cut it anymore." — JD Albert, Director of Engineering, Bresslergroup

"If it gets your team and your users talking and the constructive criticism can flow, then your wireframe is doing its job in uncovering better solutions." — Shaun O'Connell, Web Developer, Abletech

"A wireframe is meant to communicate and test. You want to do the least amount of work required to fulfill those functions. Anything more is a waste of time and resources." — Giff Constable, CEO, Neo

Minimum Viable Product

One defining element of the *Lean Startup* method is the need to go to the customer, early and often. *Entrepreneurs* following this approach will often bring along their **minimum viable product** (**MVP**)—the first version of a product that demonstrates an ability to fulfill the *startup's value proposition* to any extent. It is the most simple or basic (i.e., minimum) product instance that can still perform the required functions (i.e., viable).

The motivation for an MVP is to allow a company to move forward faster by avoiding spending months, if not years, tweaking its product before the public ever even sees it. There's no need to build out all potential features of the product that could serve some user in some situation, when a bare bones version enables learning and may even be adequate for early adopters. An extreme MVP, in which much of the processing is done by humans rather than being automated, is (for obvious reasons) known as a **Wizard of Oz MVP**.

It is by no means obvious what to include in an MVP and what to leave out. It is best to keep in mind that the MVP is a vehicle to maximize validated learning for the least amount of time and effort. An MVP should thus focus on resolving the highest risks faced by the *startup* as efficiently as possible. Ideally, an MVP will be designed to answer a single important question about feasibility or usability. Otherwise, the urge to keep adding features may be too great to resist. When looked at this way in the context of *Agile development*, there isn't just one MVP—rather, every *iteration* is another MVP. By shifting the focus of development from the *entrepreneur's* view of the problem and its solution to the customers and their needs, an MVP encourages a *startup* to focus on what really matters.

Example sentences:

We're focusing right now on getting our MVP together.

Because user experience was critical to the product's success, work on the MVP was focused on the system's front end.

What they called an MVP could have been an entire product line.

Quotes:

"The first step is figuring out the problem that needs to be solved and then developing a minimum viable product (MVP) to begin the process of learning as quickly as possible." — Eric Ries, Author, *The Lean Startup*

"Although the [Lean Startup] methodology is just a few years old, its concepts—such as 'minimum viable product' and 'pivoting'—have quickly taken root in the start-up world, and business schools have already begun adapting their curricula to teach them." — Steve Blank, Author, *The Startup Owner's Manual*

"A successful minimum viable product helps you start the learning process as soon as possible, and not just to answer the technical questions of 'how' but also to eliminate the business uncertainty of 'why.'" — Chris Bank, Marketing Lead, Tactile

"By now, the concepts popularized by Eric Ries' *The Lean Startup* have become part of everyday startup lingo. With that, the implications of each concept are misconstrued and [lose] meaning. MVP is used to describe the first version of a product *launch*, which it is not. Pivot is used loosely when teams abandon an idea on a whim in favor of another idea. Talking to customers is understood as asking your friends and peers what they think about your idea." — Grace Ng, Co-founder & Creative Director, Javelin

Pivot

The term **pivot**, introduced in 2009 by Eric Ries of *Lean Startup* fame, refers to a significant evidence-based change in business vision or strategy that retains its roots in the original approach. Unlike a jump, a pivot suggests a change in direction, and one during which contact is maintained with the ground—a change with continuity. Ideally, it should be possible to redirect much of the work already done toward different ends.

What kind of situation calls for a pivot? One might be when the first vision for a product isn't being realized as well as the *founding team* had anticipated, but new information emerges through the feedback loop about an entirely different—and incidental—aspect of the business that is working (or has the potential to work) extremely well. A pivot would be to change the direction of the business to emphasize this new aspect and/or capitalize on a new market opportunity.

The pivot is the exercise of the scientific method in product development. If the hypothesis embedded in an *MVP* does not pan out (on the basis of customer reactions, usage statistics, etc.), a pivot takes the form of an appropriate modification to that hypothesis, which can become the basis of a revised *MVP*.

Ries elaborates that a pivot might try to solve a different problem for the same *market* segment (a customer problem pivot) or a similar problem for a different *market* segment (a segment pivot), or it might zoom in on a specific feature of the current product and make it the focus of the company's strategy (a feature pivot).

Perseverance and adaptability both have their place as virtues. Shifting with the latest fad and stubbornly plodding ahead with only minor corrections can each lead a *startup* to its demise. Determining when to try harder, pivot, or throw in the towel can be among the hardest decisions; running experiments and carefully analyzing the results can help, as can measuring performance against plans.

Example sentences:

They pivoted to take advantage of the latest trend in streaming video.

Six months post-launch, they pivoted on their target demographic.

After the venture's third pivot, the VC was certain that it lacked focus.

Quotes:

"Unless you achieve instantaneous overnight success, you will be faced [with] difficult decisions. Pivot or persevere? Add features or remove them? Charge money or give it away for free? Freemium or subscription or advertising?" — Eric Ries, Author, *The Lean Startup*

"You quit when you can't find any customers, you stick when all signs point upward and you pivot when your customers keep asking you [to]." — Matt MacNaughton, Co-founder & CEO, PromoJam and Culture Jam Inc.

"If you're still passionate, and still obsessed, always try a pivot before quitting." — Brenden Mulligan, Founder & CEO, Cluster Labs

"Constant pivoting is like having a compass with no bearing. You need to know true north." — Mike Moritz, Chairman, Sequoia Partners

"I love the result of our pivot. I also love the idea of pivoting. But I have a problem with the word 'pivot.' The action sounds surgical, near-instant, and tidy. The actual experience is nothing like that. Instead, our pivot was more like a weeks-long trudge through a fog of confusion that took lots of hard work and hard choices to emerge from." — Erik Larson, Founder & CEO, Cloverpop

"Often, the 'pivot until you succeed' approach appeals to technologists who are in love with their tech. You get your technology into the market and see who wants it." — Henry Kressel and Norman Winarsky, Authors, *If You Really Want to Change the World*

User Experience

User experience, aka **UX,** covers all aspects of a person's interaction—behaviors, attitudes, and emotions—with a company's products or services. Commonly incorrectly used as synonymous with **user interface**, aka **UI**, user experience is broader. UX encompasses UI because the interface element is the user's contact point with the company's offering. The UX usage serves to place the evaluative emphasis subjectively on the connection between product and customer, rather than objectively on the product.

The term was popularized in the mid 1990's by Don Norman, who felt it was important to expand on the existing field of usability engineering to include a more holistic development approach to encompass the user's needs, motivations, and values. Getting to the user's exact needs with the least amount of "fuss and bother," not to mention confusion, as well as his second priority of "simplicity and elegance," summarize Norman's feelings about UX. In reality the user experience umbrella, on the pragmatic level of execution, involves the need for cross-functional elements, e.g. design, graphics, systems, engineering, information architecture, and user interface, to converge.

Norman believed that a good user experience is the product of a **user-centered design** (UCD) process that focuses primarily on the needs, expectations, and context of the actual users of a system, rather than deriving the system's interactions with them from the broader goals of the business or, worse, the capabilities of the underlying technology, and forcing them to adapt. UCD may involve defining **persona** archetypes for various types of users, as well as variations on *use cases* and *usage scenarios*.

There is no doubt about the concept's significance within the *startup* culture, leading some *VCs* and *startup* mentors to posit that along with a business person and an engineer, a UX designer is the third must-have on a *startup* team.

Example sentences:

The underlying technology is good, but they really need to improve their website's user experience.

We're applying UCD to optimize our product's UX.

User experience is not just about creating beautiful interfaces.

Quotes:

"I invented the term (user experience design) because I thought human interface and usability were too narrow. I wanted to cover all aspects of the person's experience with the system including industrial design, graphics, the interface, the physical interaction, and the manual." — Don Norman, Co-founder, Nielsen Norman Group

"I'm talking particularly about consumer tech, where the user experience and the brand is so important for differentiating from all the other crap..." — Enrique Allen, Founder, The Designer Fund

"You cannot NOT have a user experience." — Lou Carbone, Author, *Clued In*

"User interfaces have to do with people, and computer scientists don't like to work on problems involving people. The classic work on user interfaces that sets the current paradigm was invented outside of universities in industrial research laboratories and government-funded institutes." — Stuart Card, Consulting Professor, Stanford University

"User experience is at the core of everything, or should be. Those two words ('user' and 'experience') should be considered independently, as well as together. Who's your user, and what are they experiencing when they find you?" — Caleb Ludwick, Director, 26 Tools

API

API, an acronym of **application programming interface**, refers to a set of protocols through which programmers can access external services (from other programs), which may query proprietary data, access sensors or actuators, or perform computations. In essence, an API acts as a library of pre-established communication links that allows a developer to build a computer program that "talks" with a different computer program in order to make use of a desired service.

Without good APIs, Google maps, Yelp reviews, and YouTube videos would not be so ubiquitous, it would be impossible to copy text from Microsoft Word and paste it to Facebook, and movie tickets could not be purchased via mobile app.

"API" may also refer to the means of accessing a **software development kit** (**SDK**), which provides programming tools or libraries as well as any documents a company believes will simplify a developer's job.

An API can be sold or made available for free; the latter is an intermediate step with less risk than an *open source* approach, in that functionality is shared, but not its implementation. An API can also be seen as an intermediate step towards a *platform*, making a more constrained set of options available to its users.

Using another firm's API can save programming effort and provide reach through the provider's network, but also creates dependence on the provider, to whom control is ceded. Offering an API allows the firm to distribute a tightly defined set of its functionality through an unbounded number of channels at the cost of an investment in maintenance.

Example sentences:

Ted really liked working with that API because it cut down his programming time considerably.

By opening their API, they are hoping to encourage the development of an ecosystem around their product.

His company put together a poor API and received complaints that it was causing some apps to function improperly.

Quotes:

"As scalable infrastructure is increasingly composed from and defined by services, high performance API management becomes a must-have characteristic." — Stephen O'Grady, Co-founder & Principal Analyst, RedMonk

"The current definition of web APIs has jumped out of the SOA toolbox in the last 10 years, focusing on the simple, meaningful access of common business and government resources. This has allowed APIs to be effectively put to use across every business sector, by startups, SMBs, the enterprise and even government agencies." — Kin Lane, API Evangelist

"When you open up your iPhone so many of the applications on there are driven by APIs." — Travis Todd, Co-founder, FullContact

"Facebook has released a secret software development kit (SDK) to select developers that allows them to build chat bots for the Facebook Messenger app..." — Michael Grothaus, Writer, *Fast Company*

Open Source

Open source is a development model that actively encourages universal access to technology. By making software open source, the *copyright* holder grants the public the right to study, alter, and re-distribute it. Open-source projects select from various standard licenses that limit, in different ways, what people may do with the code after downloading it. For instance, licensers might not allow closed-source modifications to the code. Often, many people are contributing, simultaneously and without much advanced coordination, to open-source projects. This phenomenon is enabled by decentralized **version control**, which allows people to work independently on different aspects of a project without unnecessarily interfering with one another and also allows existing projects to spawn new ones, so that they can evolve in multiple directions.

In addition to the obvious lower cost, open-source software provides other advantages to companies that choose to use it, including better reliability and security (open-source software is reviewed by significantly more people for these concerns than is proprietary software) and the assurance that the company can modify the code, if necessary, or else leave with its data.

Perhaps surprisingly, a growing *business model* involves commercially bundling, servicing, developing tools around, and training customers to use open-source software packages.

Technology companies have come to understand the value of investing in open-source projects. Benefits include access to or influence over the development of the technology, improved public relations as a leader in the field, the efforts of (and an opportunity to recruit) the best practitioners, and potentially a widely-used infrastructure that supports its intended products.

Example sentences:

To save funds, the startup uses open-source wherever possible.

The investor was suspicious of their open-source business model.

In supporting the open-source project, the firm hoped to create a widely used platform well-suited to its gaming technology.

Quotes:

"In Silicon Valley, innovation is the fertilizer that makes the crops grow. With open source, software is more like topsoil, and those who nurture that soil believe they prosper longer than those who just throw fertilizer on it." — Dana Blankenhorn, Blogger, *ZDNet*

"While open-source developers can be as faddish as the next person, one of the cardinal tenets of open source is that it encourages developers to 'scratch their own itches'. In other words, solve pressing problems that they may have, regardless of venture funding." — Matt Asay, VP Mobile, Adobe

"I have very seldom seen a program that has worked well enough for my needs, and having sources available can be a life-saver." — Linus Torvalds, Fellow, Linux Foundation

"Certainly there's a phenomenon around open source. You know free software will be a vibrant area. There will be a lot of neat things that get done there." — Bill Gates, Co-chair, Bill & Melinda Gates Foundation

"The risk of open source is that you have no intellectual property." — Nick Heudecker, Research Director, Gartner

Cybersecurity

Cybersecurity is the protection of computer systems, networks and devices from unauthorized access and the resultant possibility of destruction or theft of data. Computer systems controlling anything from government secrets to financial records to physical infrastructure are currently vulnerable.

Black hat *hackers* seeking money, notoriety, or to satisfy a political or religious ideology maliciously breach computers or networks to steal data or money, delete data, or usurp authority. **White hat** *hackers* may be paid consultants who, in **penetration tests**, attempt to break into a system in a controlled and protected way. Rather than exploiting the weakness, a white hat alerts the responsible party so the breach can be corrected. The terms come from old Western movies, where bad guys wear black hats and good guys wear white. **Gray hats** exist in a murky region between those extremes; such people may break into a system without permission in hope of either fixing it for a fee or publicly disclosing the vulnerability.

Attackers often place malicious code called **malware** on a target system. A **Trojan**, based on the story of the Greek invasion of Troy, is an innocent-looking package that carries a dangerous payload. A **backdoor** is an undocumented vulnerability often intentionally placed for maintenance purposes. In a new twist on malware, **ransomware** locks down that system until a payment is made. Viruses are insidious malware that, like the biological variety, replicate themselves, in some cases creating a botnet of connected computers well-suited to disguising illegal activity. The vulnerabilities whereby attackers can access common systems are known as **exploits**. **Zero day exploits**, those exploits that have not yet been publicly revealed, are in high demand among product manufacturers, criminals, and government spies and are traded in a shadowy marketplace.

Promising approaches for **online security** are multilayered. They include **encrypting** user data and messages to prevent them from being read without authorization as well as **intrusion detection systems (IDS), or**

better, intrusion prevention systems (IPS) that go far beyond matching patterns of malware to monitor and protect system internals. But as long as companies and governments insist on maintaining their respective access to user data, our systems will remain vulnerable.

Example sentences:

Every company should have a comprehensive cybersecurity plan.

Regretting the damage caused by his earlier cyberadventures, he has reformed to wear a white hat.

Our cybersecurity protocols were put to the test last year when a vulnerability was revealed in our network database.

Quotes:

"Cryptography forms the basis for trust online. By deliberately undermining online security in a short-sighted effort to eavesdrop, the NSA is undermining the very fabric of the Internet." — Bruce Schneier, Fellow, Berkman Center for Internet & Society, Harvard University

"If you are a purist; you can say there is a difference between information security and cyber security, but if you are a practitioner they are one and the same—[it's] still simply about protecting data/information—digital or not." — Ken Shaurette, Director IT Services, FIPCO

"Our entire modern way of life, from communication to commerce to conflict, depends on the Internet, and the resultant cybersecurity issues challenge literally everyone." — Peter Singer, Strategist & Senior Fellow, The New America Foundation

"The difference between penetration testing and hacking is whether you have the system owner's permission." — Christian Kirsch, Principal Product Marketing Manager for User Insight, Rapid7

FUNDING

Bootstrapping

A *startup* that has received at least one *investment round* from a *venture capitalist* is said to be **venture-backed**. Businesses financed by *venture capital* will be high-risk and high-potential. In exchange for assuming this substantial risk to their investment, the *venture capitalist* will take an ownership position in the company.

"Pulling yourself up by your bootstraps" is an Old English saying that refers to the laces (or straps) on one's boots, and the use of these to move the entire boot forward (perhaps literally out of the mud). It indicates making do with what you already have in order to have more (as in self-reliance) and is also the basis of the term "boot" as applied to starting a computer (using primitive systems to initialize more complex ones).

In Silicon Valley, **bootstrapping** has come to denote a *founding team* self-funding their venture. The *startup* may forgo angel and venture backing entirely, or, as in the case of eBay, bootstrap for several years while developing market traction.

Venture funding can mean giving up majority control to the investors, even at an *A-round*. The *VC firms* will generally get at least one *board* seat, collectively. If things don't go well, *founders* may find themselves out of the picture altogether. While venture backing can allow a company to *scale* more rapidly than any alternative financial source, finding investors and keeping them satisfied can be a significant drain on resources that may distract from the fundamentals of the business. Many *founders* see bootstrapping as an attractive alternative, particularly as the costs of starting up continue to decline.

Example sentences:

Bootstrapping was not difficult for her because she had a financial background and knew how to measure and evaluate her business expenses versus the cash flow needs.

He was not able to bootstrap his company as he needed a high six-figure capital outlay to purchase equipment for his concept.

Sue bootstrapped her business because she did not want to have to generate returns on the schedule that VCs would demand.

Quotes:

"Frankly, I don't think most people are willing to make the sacrifices that you need to make to be an entrepreneur and to bootstrap a company from nothing." — Christian Chabot, Co-founder & CEO, Tableau Software

"I am a bootstrapper. I have initiative and insight and guts, but not much money. I keep my focus on growing the business—not on politics, career advancement, or other wasteful distractions." — Seth Godin, Author, *The Bootstrapper's Manifesto*

"The slow bootstrap worked really well [for GoPro], and the smoke-and-tires approach worked for Pebble. ... As long as you can bootstrap, not at the sacrifice of competitive advantage, bootstrapping is a really powerful thing because it allows you to be totally devoted to your vision." — Nick Woodman, CEO, GoPro

"I think this is the magic number for venture-backed SaaS is: By Year 4, your revenues need to be $20m or more, growing 100% or more, to really make it." — Jason M. Lemkin, Managing Director, Storm Ventures

Friends and Family

Where might the *founder* of a company look first for investment capital, before turning to more traditional sources such as *angels* or *VCs*? Typically, to those with whom he or she is closest—friends and family.

There are pluses and minuses to this approach. Should your venture fail, your relationships with the friends and family who invested could be irreparably damaged. On the other hand, an *entrepreneur* may be more assiduous with a friend or family member's cash than with money from someone they don't know. The biggest reason to go to friends and family is that at such an early stage, more sophisticated investors may consider the company too risky— some extend the label to **friends, family, and fools**—and, indeed, over 90% of such early ventures will fail. On the rare chance that your *startup* does well, your friends and family will wish they had been asked to participate.

Friends and family *rounds* usually raise $25,000 to $250,000 in total— the amount, of course, depending on whom your friends and family are. For some companies, this may be enough to build their *prototype* or to put together their *crowdfunding* campaign and video.

Startups can be extremely difficult to *value*, even for professional investors, so friends and family rounds usually take the form of **convertible notes**, i.e., debt entitling the holder to convert to *equity* upon a later, *priced investment round*, buying in at some discount to the share price at that round and placing a cap on the *valuation* that they must ultimately pay. But this formulation demands care in setting both expectations and legal requirements for repayment in the event that the venture fails. In the words of *entrepreneur* and investor Adeo Ressi, "It's ridiculous that the primary way to 'invest' in startups is to straddle them with debt through short-term loans. We are bankrupting the future out of the gate, and it's time that we change this." He and others have proposed alternative means of *startup* funding.

Example sentences:

Not having made enough progress to impress angel investors, the startup was forced to go back for a second friends and family round.

She selected her aunt to participate in her friends and family round, thinking she was best able to afford to lose the investment if the venture did not succeed.

The high discount he offered in the friends and family round scared off seed investors.

Quotes:

"Many tech entrepreneurs take investment from friends and family to test the viability of an idea. They raise just enough to fund a developer's salary, office space, monthly rent, and a steady supply of ramen noodle soup." — Christina Farr, Senior Writer, *Fast Company*

"The advantage of raising money from friends and family is that they're easy to find. You already know them." — Paul Graham, Co-founder, Y Combinator

"Raising money from your friends and family is a decent indicator that you can successfully convince someone to believe and invest in you." — Dan Reich, Co-founder & CEO, Troops

"Well meaning, but inexperienced, entrepreneurs often treat their friends and family investors unfairly and cause considerable damage to their startup and future funding opportunities." — Basil Peters, Author, *Early Exits*

"I don't know for sure, but I would suspect that friends and family make up the largest source of funding for entrepreneurs and startups." — Fred Wilson, Co-founder, Union Square Ventures

Crowdfunding

Crowdfunding is the process of funding a new project or business by raising money from a multitude of people, often unknown to the *entrepreneur,* who make large or small investments in the new venture.

The crowdfunding model has three components: the initiator, who proposes the idea to be funded; the people who provide funds to support the idea, known as **backers**; and a "matchmaker" organization that brings the two together. Typically the matchmaker is a web site dedicated to that purpose.

Two of the most prominent crowdfunding firms are Indiegogo and Kickstarter. Through crowdfunding campaigns of set durations (typically a month), the initiators, whether individuals or companies, seek supporters who pledge funds at various levels to support creative projects or new product ideas. Rewards are set at each level, and may vary from receiving a copy of the finished product to a special, perhaps public, "thank-you." Some crowdfunding sites specialize in raising contributions for nonprofits. *Startups* may use crowdfunding as a form of market validation (and demonstration of their prowess in selling non-existent product).

The next frontier of crowdfunding is to use the concept for raising *startup* investment capital. In April 2012, the Federal government passed the **Jumpstart Our Business Startups Act (JOBS Act)** to loosen certain securities regulations that otherwise prevent such **equity crowdfunding** of *startups*. Regulations and customs are still being refined, but several online sites already enable accredited investors to invest in *startup equity*. Once the JOBS Act is fully in effect, anybody will be able to invest, within limits, like an *angel*. It may take some time, however, for traditional investors to be comfortable investing alongside a *crowd*.

Example sentences:

He's planning to crowdfund production of his new product.

Crowdfunding gives backers the opportunity to participate in the creative process.

Crowdfunding for startups sounds like a great idea, but I'm not sure I want to have 1,000 shareholders.

Quotes:

"A fun fact that most people don't know is that the Statue of Liberty was crowd funded." — Erica Labovitz, Category Business Director, Film, Indiegogo

"What my editors ... were intelligent enough to note is that crowdfunding provides a final persuasive link in the crowdsourcing argument." — Jeff Howe, Author, *Crowdsourcing: Why the Power of the Crowd is Driving the Future of Business*

"Perhaps crowdfunding can help restore the magic—by freeing entrepreneurship from the taint of Big Finance." — Reihan Salam, Executive Editor, *National Review*

"Right now entrepreneurs are using crowdfunding to raise hundreds of thousands of dollars in pure donations—imagine the possibilities if these small dollar donors became investors with a stake in the venture." — Barack Obama, President, The United States of America

"It ended up being a giant dog's breakfast of different bills combined together, and then some genius, probably some congressional staffer, said "How are we gonna get this thing to pass? Oh—let's say it has something to do with jobs. Jumpstarting Our Business Startups! JOBS, JOBS!" And then, what congressperson can vote against something called the JOBS Act? It was a miracle." — Naval Ravikant, Managing Partner, Hit Forge

Accelerator

The purpose of an **accelerator** is, as the name suggests, to help fledgling *startups* accelerate their growth. Before accelerators there were **incubators**, which began as early as 1959. Accelerators and incubators both provide varying levels of growth support to a *startup*, the primary difference between the two being that accelerators tend to have set program durations.

The route into an accelerator typically starts with a competitive application process. Some popular accelerators have acceptance rates as low as 1%. The accelerator usually makes an investment (typically between $20,000 and $50,000) in the selected *startups* (known collectively as a **cohort**). During the program term, they participate in educational programs and receive advice from mentors. Each member *startup* is expected to refine and validate its business concept and make rapid progress in developing a company, culminating in a **Demo Day** where presentations are made to investors. The combination of learning, connections, and the recognition for participating in an accelerator can help propel a firm forward. And the programs themselves can earn a lot of money if their graduates do well.

The first accelerator was Y Combinator, started in 2005. Since then, accelerators have multiplied, and lately it seems that everyone and their brother has one. There are various specialized accelerators as well; some are restricted to female *entrepreneurs*, particular technologies, or *social entrepreneurs*. Some accelerators are associated with *collaborative workspaces*, and provide space as a benefit to the ventures. Others are associated with educational institutions, and provide access to and lectures by faculty.

From their perspective, *VCs* are being asked to pay a premium (in terms of higher *valuation*) for *startups* that come out of a big-name accelerator. Are graduating *startups* really better, or just more polished? To the extent that "polish" is a key success factor, it may not be a meaningful distinction.

Example sentences:

My experience with the accelerator was worth the equity stake that I gave up.

The best feature of my experience with the accelerator was the bonds I formed with other startups in my cohort.

Many billion-dollar startups got their start in accelerators.

Quotes:

"Essentially, the function of an accelerator is to turn the art of starting a company into a program that can be repeated, churning out valuable companies as if on an assembly line." — Dani Fankhauser, Co-founder, ReadThisNext

"Accelerators help venture capital firms by forcing entrepreneurs to 'fail fast,' and truly understand their risks before they even consider raising venture capital." — David T. Morgenthaler, Founding Partner, Morgenthaler Ventures

"Every month hundreds of startups in the United States apply to accelerator and incubator programs. Their hope is that acceptance will grant them access to the wise mentorship, industry connections and money that will lead them to the promised land." — Karsten Strauss, Staff Writer, *Forbes*

"Those who tend to outperform when they graduate from incubators likely would have made it without them." — Erin Griffith, Writer, *Fortune*

"Today the accelerator held [its] inaugural class demo day (think graduation meets show-and-tell) at New York City's IAC headquarters, featuring ten new technology companies focused on education." — Marisa Kaplan, Creator & Writer, *EdGeeks*

Equity

Equity consists of claims to the net assets of a firm and any future return the firm may generate. Equity in a *startup* is generally obtained by the direct purchase or receipt of stock or by the exercise of *employee stock options*. *Startup* equity can be paid for by cash investment or by contribution of labor (so-called **sweat equity**).

A corporation's number of **authorized shares** is the maximum amount of stock that it may issue. **Issued shares** are those authorized shares that have been issued, or allocated, to shareholders. **Shares outstanding** are those issued shares held outside the company, as opposed to **treasury shares** held by the corporation itself. Treasury shares have no exercisable rights.

Common stock is generally held by employees and, ultimately, the general public. **Restricted common stock** is compensation offered to an employee in the form of company stock that has not yet *vested*. This stock is non-transferrable, has no privileges, and is subject to reclamation by the company in the condition that it fails to *vest*, but is considered to have been issued to stockholders. *Employee stock options* may be similarly restricted. *Founder's stock* is a privileged form of restricted common stock.

Preferred stock is held by *VCs* and, possibly, *angel investors*. It differs from common stock in that it can give the holder a claim to additional dividends as well as the right to receive dividends and proceeds of *liquidation* or sale before common shareholders receive similar distributions. Traditionally, preferred stock does not give holders the right to vote on company issues but in Silicon Valley it can often be voted as if it had been converted to common, i.e., on an **as converted** basis. The conversion is initially one-to-one, but may be more generous if the common stock has been *diluted*.

Echoing a past boom, equity is the sand through which people at every echelon in Silicon Valley now sift, seeking their share of gold.

Example sentences:

The VCs took their usual 30% equity stake in the company.

The founder's equity has been diluted by three financing events.

The co-founders spent much of their time arguing over equity.

Quotes:

"Equity compensation—getting a piece of the company—is one of the defining aspects of working at a startup. It is attractive not only for its perceived monetary value, but for the sense of ownership it gives employees." — Conner Forrest, Enterprise Editor, *TechRepublic*

"The people you want to attract to your business are the people who want equity. You need people who are willing to take risks. And then you need to reward them." — Bill Harris, CEO, Personal Capital

"One of the most common questions I get is about how equity should be distributed. I'll warn you in advance: There are no hard and fast rules. Equity is negotiated on a case-by-case basis, which makes it hard to give any generalizations." — Stever Robbins, CEO Advisor & Consultant, Stever Robbins, Inc.

"Don't think in terms of number of shares or the valuation of shares when you join an early-stage startup. Think of yourself as a late-stage founder and negotiate for a specific equity percentage ownership in the company. You should base this percentage on your anticipated contribution to the company's growth in value." — Mary Russell, Attorney, Stock Option Counsel

"When you're getting started, sweat equity is often a critical component of your negotiating leverage with co-founders, early stage employees and others who aren't paid market wages to help you grow your business." — Asheesh Advani, CEO, JA Worldwide

Vesting

Vesting is the practice of awarding *equity* (stock or *stock options*) in a *startup* to an employee or other contributor over a period of time rather than all at once. It serves to keep early employees (or *co-founders*) of a company from unfairly leaving with their *equity* before their proportional share of the work required to build a company has been completed. Vesting is a process through which one becomes invested in the firm.

Equity normally vests gradually during the vesting period. Stock or options that have not vested are *restricted*. As *equity* vests, the employee receives control of more, and eventually all, of his or her shares, after which time the equity is said to be **fully vested**. While any at-will employee is subject to termination without cause, *clawing back* unvested stock via this threat is frowned upon.

Vesting cliffs enable a *startup* to offer *equity* on a trial basis. If the relationship ends by action of either party during the trial period, i.e., before reaching the cliff, then the departing party receives no *equity*. A typical **vesting schedule** is four years monthly with a one-year cliff, meaning that a quarter of the *equity* is granted after the first year and one forty-eighth of the *equity* is granted each month thereafter.

Vesting can be accelerated by certain events. **Single trigger acceleration** requires only a single event, generally transfer of control of the company. **Acceleration of vesting** may also be full or partial, depending on how much *equity* vests upon the event. Advisors to a firm, for example, receive "**full acceleration** on *exit*," meaning that if the company is sold before the vesting period has ended, they immediately receive rights to the remainder of the *equity* promised to them. Severance clauses may separately allow for only **partial acceleration** upon termination without cause. **Double trigger acceleration** is preferred by *VCs* as it requires both transfer of control and termination without cause, making the company more attractive to potential acquirers.

Example sentences:

Because he was let go prior to the one-year cliff in his contract, he received no equity.

The company she worked for was acquired in its second year by a larger corporation, which allowed her to become fully vested in her stock due to single trigger acceleration.

In the fluid labor market, the small startup company used vesting of equity to incentivize new hires to remain with the firm for multiple years.

Quotes:

"In essence, vesting protects founders from each other and aligns incentives so everybody focuses towards a common goal: building a successful company." — Güimar Vaca Sittic, Head of Investments, FJ Labs

"Vesting is for the benefit of the company, meaning the shareholders collectively, so that they can retain talent and so that ownership does not exit in the hands of those who haven't contributed long-term." — Gil Silberman, CLO, Equidate

"Accelerated vesting of equity is messy. The point is to incent people to stay through the 4 years it takes to succeed. Accelerate the vesting, and you remove the incentive." — Kamal Hassan, CEO, IncMind, Founder Institute Toronto

"Founder vesting is founder friendly, the exact opposite of what most people think. It keeps the balance between working founders, who build the company up, and absent founders, who leave early." — Dan Shapiro, CEO, Glowforge

Pitch

A **pitch** is any type of persuasive presentation meant to elicit interest, excitement, financial investment, or sales leads related to a product, person, idea, business, or project. Pitches can be as formal as a rehearsed multimedia presentation or as informal as a conversation over a meal. A pitch can last for several hours or be as short as several seconds (as in an *elevator pitch*). Pitch, as a verb, refers to the act of giving someone your pitch. A good pitch is considered essential for *startups* to attract investors or partners.

A *startup*'s pitch to investors will cover the problem addressed, the solution applied, the people involved and their qualifications, the *business model* and formula for *monetization*, and a sense of the size of the opportunity, along with arguments supporting all of the above. Intangibles are also expected, including confidence, charisma, and demonstrated understanding of industry competitors and the market.

The elements of a *startup*'s pitch will be combined into a **pitch deck**, typically a set of PowerPoint slides, used for presenting to potential investors and others. **Pitching competitions** (also called **pitch days**), where *startups* give their pitches and prizes are awarded to the best, occur frequently in Silicon Valley. *Startups* often maintain two decks: one with more explanation to be sent in advance of a presentation, and a more concise one that is used during presentations. Investor and marketing specialist Guy Kawasaki proposed the **10/20/30 Rule** for pitch decks: they should have ten slides, last no more than twenty minutes, and contain no font smaller than thirty points.

Numerous Silicon Valley consultants specialize in helping *startup founders* develop their pitch deck and polish their pitching skills. Although many will improve their technique, few can hope to approach the **reality distortion field** achieved by Steve Jobs in pitching Apple products.

Example sentences:

They pitched us their idea over coffee this morning.

She's taking a team to New York to pitch a group of investors.

I just saw a pitch for a new online game site.

Quotes:

"OK folks ... if there's ONE thing I can help you with tonight, it's how to pitch. It's very simple, and I can teach you in about five minutes. Here's the secret: PITCH THE PROBLEM, NOT THE SOLUTION." — Dave McClure, Founding Partner, 500 Startups

"A lot of people ask whether they need a deck when pitching to a VC. I don't think a deck is required, most important is telling your story. But a deck often helps in framing and structuring the story and making sure that you get through all of the key points you want to cover. ... My basic advice to people building decks is to use it to help tell a story for why you are doing this and how big you think it can be." — Josh Elman, Partner, Greylock

"For an entrepreneur, life's a pitch!" — Guy Kawasaki, Chief Evangelist, Canva and former Chief Evangelist, Apple

"Raising money from investors for your startup is challenging at any stage and requires a great pitch, even for experienced founders with significant traction in their company." — Chance Barnett, CEO, Crowdfunder

"One of the big no-no's [we learned] about early on ... is to publicly share the pitchdeck you've used to raise money. At least, not before you've been acquired or failed or in any other way been removed from [the] stage." — Dharmesh Shah, Founder & CTO, HubSpot

Elevator Pitch

You never know who you will run into in the elevator. An **elevator pitch**, sometimes called an **elevator speech**, is meant to be, quite literally, a *pitch* that can be given in the amount of time it takes an elevator to travel between floors. One uses this brief and persuasive statement to spark interest in themselves, their organization, their idea, or their product. These *pitches* are intended not to convey specific information, but rather to be so engaging that the person to whom they are delivered wants to hear more—whatever the topic.

Generally, a person has their elevator pitch at the ready so that they can present themselves effectively should they unexpectedly find themselves in the presence of someone they would like to impress. Since elevators pitches are given, at least supposedly, with no advance notice to either the deliverer or the recipient, people spend considerable amounts of time practicing and perfecting their speech to ensure that they can spit it out quickly at any time.

An effective elevator pitch impresses the listener with what the presenter can accomplish and the compelling reasons why the product or service is important as well as distinct from the rest of the market. A problem faced by one's customers and the related *pain points* are often a focus.

It is essential that an elevator pitch limit the amount of information, lest the listener become overwhelmed and lose interest. Sixty seconds is considered the absolute maximum length for an elevator pitch, while closer to thirty seconds is ideal. Other best practices for elevator pitches include using a brief question to engage the listener, avoiding buzzwords, and not loading it down with bragging points or lists of product features.

Example sentences:

He knew his elevator pitch was effective when the VC asked him a few questions about his venture.

She practiced her elevator pitch until it was perfect.

His elevator pitch was so good that it landed him a meeting with the VC he ran into on the golf course.

Quotes:

"I have found that an effective elevator pitch is nine things: concise, clear, compelling, credible, conceptual, concrete, consistent, customized, conventional." — Chris O'Leary, Author, *Elevator Pitch Essentials*

"Think of the elevator pitch as an executive summary that provides a quick overview of your business and details why you are going to be successful." — Noah Parsons, COO, Palo Alto Software

"The elevator pitch—so named because it should last no longer than the average elevator ride—is far too important to take casually. It's one of the most effective methods available to reach new buyers and clients with a winning message." — Aileen Pincus, President, The Pincus Group

"The purpose of an elevator pitch to an investor is to excite him or her about THE BUSINESS CASE OF YOUR CONCEPT. The business case is about 'Who will pay how much for what and to whom.'" — Prajakt Raut, Founder, The Hub for Startups

"Every entrepreneur needs a value proposition statement for his or her startup that can hook potential investors and partners in less than a minute—the short time you might join them in an elevator on the way to their offices. This may sound easy, but every investor I know is frustrated by wasted time listening to rambling, emotional pitches that are not to the point." — Martin Zwillig, Founder & CEO, Startup Professionals

Exponential Growth

Any quantity that grows by a fixed percent at regular intervals is said to exhibit **exponential growth**. The change at each **interval** is known as the **growth factor**. Compound interest, for example, is an exponential growth scenario. The archetypal Silicon Valley example is **Moore's Law**, which describes how the number of transistors on a chip has doubled approximately every two years. The converse—**exponential decay**—occurs when the growth factor is less than one.

In *startup* culture, the key for discerning *value* is whether the entity has the potential for exponential growth. In fact, according to Paul Graham, Co-founder of Y Combinator, the term *startup* in its purest form relates specifically to new companies whose product has the ability to experience exponential growth. He defines a *startup* as a company designed to grow fast continuously, as opposed to one which may grow fast initially but ultimately taper off. Not all businesses that are *startups* must be about technology, but they must be about exponential growth. For other businesses, growth is constrained in ways that preclude that type of *scaling*. And indeed, some *founders* intentionally limit the growth of their firm, deciding instead to create a **lifestyle business**, which sustains a desired level of income while leaving them with some free time.

Exponential growth is visualized as a "**hockey-stick curve**," indicating an initial period of seemingly slow growth followed by overwhelming growth after an **inflection point** (the bend in the hockey-stick). When looking for companies to invest in, *VCs* tend to look for exponential growth, rather than linear growth, as a sign that the company has *unicorn* potential. But in the presence of an inflection point, timing (whether one is on one side of the bend or the other) is everything.

Example sentences:

We grew exponentially, acquiring new customers at a consistent rate of 7% a week.

The exponential growth we experienced was attributed to the "sharing" function we built into our model.

We watched in horror as our exponential growth turned into exponential decay as people posted about their bad experiences.

The founder was shocked to realize that their exponential growth was limited by the small market size.

Quotes:

"Our ancestors must rarely have encountered cases of exponential growth, because our intuitions are no guide here. What happens to fast growing startups tends to surprise even the founders." — Paul Graham, Co-founder, Y Combinator

"Predicting that a change will happen in '3-5 years' is easy, but it's more rewarding to think about what events will create the changes. Step-change events signal investment opportunities that lead to exponential growth, rather than trendline growth, and provide the foundation for outsized returns." — Taylor Davidson, Managing Director, Unstructured Ventures

"The key is this, build a business that you can demonstrate exponential growth. VC's aren't investing in a restaurant, they're investing in the recipe and ability to scale. If you raised $2mil then you should be able to leverage that for 20x–50x growth." — Brian Dear, Founder, iCouch.me

"The only way to generate sustained exponential growth is to make whatever you're making sufficiently good." — Sam Altman, President, Y Combinator

Due Diligence

In its most general sense, **due diligence** refers to informing oneself through deep evaluation of material information in order to make the most considered and enlightened decision on whether or not to take a course of action. The goal is to reveal the costs, the benefits, and, especially, the risks.

This term came into common use after the passage of the Securities and Exchange Act of 1933, which led to greater regulatory observance of broker-dealer firms and the first surveillance over brokers' investment recommendations to clients. Those firms that could demonstrate having undertaken a process of due diligence in presenting investment ideas to their clients were permitted to proceed by the SEC. In this case, full disclosure to the client was achieved by gathering exhaustive research on the business entity or stock and then making that information completely accessible to the client.

In the *startup* world, due diligence might take place in various scenarios. One is when investors courted by a *startup* begin to seriously consider investing. The other is when a company begins to seriously consider acquiring another company. In either case, the potential investor or acquirer performs due diligence by obtaining and evaluating information regarding the company in question. Information is obtained via a deep-dive search for risks related to the company, its operations, its accounting, its customers, its staff, and so on. This scrupulously thorough check is used as a means to prevent overpaying in a deal or, perhaps, prevent making a bad deal altogether. Especially in the case of *VCs*, due diligence may involve *back-channeling*. Due diligence can take place in other situations where much is at stake as well, such as prior to hiring a key executive.

Investors prefer that *founders* disclose any serious problems with their *startup* in advance—but will not likely leave much to chance or trust.

Example sentences:

In the course of due diligence, it was uncovered that the venture was likely to be sued by a disgruntled former employee.

The extra effort needed to conduct a lengthy due diligence process was well worth the time.

He has been called upon to lead many due diligence efforts, including those related to mergers and acquisitions.

Quotes:

"Standard SV practice: Investor signs term sheet, does confirmatory Due Diligence, and funds at those terms unless DD surfaces deception." — Marc Andreessen, General Partner, Andreessen Horowitz

"Due diligence consists of a product review, customer references, executive team references, financial modeling, market analysis and competitive analysis." — Sean Jacobsohn, Investor, Norwest Venture Partners

"It's important to conduct your own due diligence on a startup before you write a check. You shouldn't only rely on a great pitch, or assume others are doing the due diligence for you." — Bill Clark, CEO, MicroAngel Capital Partners

"Many entrepreneurs I know underestimate the importance of their small and large actions during due diligence and the signals their behavior send to the VCs. In truth, the due diligence process itself is a gauntlet that tests the entrepreneur and informs the VC about their mettle and whether they have the character and skills to build a great company." — Jeffrey Bussgang, General Partner, Flybridge Capital

Round of Funding

A **round of funding**, or **investment round**, refers to a grouping of investments in a *startup* over a limited time frame and under similar *terms*, each potentially including multiple investors.

Early in its search for external investment, the *startup* will likely approach *friends and family* or *angel investors*. This process may evolve to a **seed round** including a *syndicate* with early-stage *venture capital firms*. The goal is to provide enough capital with which to assemble a management team, build a *prototype*, test *proof-of-concept*, or do whatever is most needed to propel the company toward milestones for attracting further investment. The seed round is usually kept small to avoid unnecessary *dilution* of the *founding team*, and because *valuation* at this point is still very subjective. A **priced investment round** is any one for which a *valuation* is set and used to transfer *equity*.

Future rounds of funding are generally received from institutional *VC firms*. The first of these is called the **Series A round**, referring to the Series A *preferred stock* issued to the investors. At this critical stage, the firm will usually raise $2-10M for a 20-40% stake. This A round is expected to last six months to two years.

Successive rounds of funding occur based on evidence of continued development, viability, and validation via increasingly quantitative metrics of the firm's progress.

In each successive round, a new **class** of *preferred stock* is issued, the *capitalization table* extended, and the letter incremented. Hence we arrive at a **Series B round** potentially followed by **Series C**, and so on.

None of this is intended as a precise formula. For example, either *crowdfunding* or **strategic investment** by established industry partners are always possible.

Example sentences:

The entrepreneur was feeling pretty good after completing her A round.

VCs are starting to expect more development before entering into an A round than they had in the past.

He was relying on that next round of funding for liquidity.

Quotes:

"An investment 'round' is simply a set of one or more investments made into a particular company, by one or more investors on essentially similar terms, and at essentially the same time." — David S. Rose, Managing Partner, Rose Tech Ventures

"Back in the early 2000s we worked with several companies who had many, many rounds of financings. I remember one that went through Series I." — Ken Maready, Founding Partner, Maready, PLLC

"Cautionary note: No competent VC is actually fooled when you show up after raising $6M in seed financing and say you're now raising an A!" — Marc Andreessen, Co-founder, Andreessen Horowitz

"It's all fun and games until you raise a Series B." — Chris Sacca, Founder & Chairman, Lowercase Capital

"What actually IS the definition of a seed vs. A-round[?] ... I think an easier definition is 'first institutional capital' which is what most A-round VCs think about what their personal funding strategies are. They want to be early and first." — Mark Suster, Partner, Upfront Ventures

Valuation

A **valuation** is an appraisal of how much a company's *equity* (assets less liabilities) is worth. No reliable methodology exists for determining the valuation of a *startup*, which by nature has limited history and an expectation of rapid growth. Estimating and discounting future cash flow (using notions of *market size* and *exit value*) can be useful, but these numbers can only be rough estimates subject to market changes, including actions of new or existing competitors (as constrained by *barriers to entry*, which will enhance valuations). Basing the value on cumulative cash expended (on the theory that the company is worth what it would cost to recreate) rewards profligacy and ignores future potential. The conventional wisdom suggests using more objective (later) valuations of comparable companies in similar *verticals* and market position at similar stages of maturation, but not every *startup* can expect to walk in Facebook's footsteps. One can compare against similar companies at a similar stage, but that gets rather circular. All of the above and numerous heuristics may be used by *startups* and investors in deciding how to price the company's *equity*. Valuations for *stock option* grants are generally more conservative than those for *investment rounds*.

What *is* clear is that the company will have considerably more assets after a major funding event than it had before. In specifying valuations around any funding event (*round of funding*), one must therefore distinguish the **pre-money valuation** (excluding the current investor's funds) from the **post-money valuation** (including those funds). **Pre-money** and **post-money** are common short forms, and these are sometimes abbreviated further as simply **pre** or **post**.

The investment amount and either form of valuation is sufficient to determine the investor's ownership percentage. By injecting $2M into a company that was $3M pre, for example, the investor now has purchased a 40% stake in an entity valued, post-money, at $5M. Since the number of shares is a large and meaningless number, the pre-money valuation stands in for the price, while the percentage ownership sold is stated in terms of the post-money valuation.

While a valuation is implied by a funding event, when *equity* is issued for other purposes the taxman will want the valuation to be backed up by a more formal appraisal process.

Example sentences:

With such a high pre-money valuation, the investor's contributed funds represented a small share of the company.

Whatever the founder said, the VCs weren't going to budge on the valuation.

Their post-money put them in the unicorn category.

Quotes:

"Valuation hinges on [entrepreneurs'] negotiating skills (which is daunting since they're going up against professional investors / negotiators). ... Unfortunately, none of the traditionally-accepted valuation methods really apply to early stage startups." — Nathan Beckord, Co-founder & CEO, Foundersuite

"So when an investor proposes an investment of $2 million at $3 million "pre" (short for [pre-money] valuation), this means that the investors will own 40% of the company after the transaction: $2m / ($3m + $2m) = 2/5 = 40%" — Brad Feld, Managing Director, Foundry Group

"I personally find that "post-money valuation" is really not nearly as useful a number as it would seem ... the 'post' part of the post-money valuation is just cash, whereas the value of the company, at least in a startup, is less about the balance sheet cash and more about the traction, product and team." — Joichi Ito, Director, MIT Media Lab

Term Sheet

The **term sheet** states all the terms and conditions of an investment or acquisition. It is not, however, the definitive or legally binding document that an entrepreneur might ultimately sign, but rather a statement of intent. In particular, after the term sheet is signed, the deal is still subject to a *due diligence* review by the investor.

The initial term sheet for an investment will normally be proposed by the *lead investor* and negotiated with the *entrepreneur*. This complex document may include (among other terms):

• Investment: how much, in how many *tranches*, at what *milestones*

• *Valuation (pre-money)*: how much the company is assumed to be worth under the deal

• *Vesting*: a schedule to be imposed on the *founding team*, even if they had been *fully vested*

• *Liquidation preference*: a multiple of the amount invested that investors insist on receiving upon *liquidation* or sale of the company, prior to payments to other stockholders

• Participation: when, upon *liquidation* or sale and after the preference payment, preferred shares should continue to be paid alongside those of other investors—either immediately (**fully participating**), after other investors are given a chance to "catch up" (**simple participating**), or never (**non-participating**—don't fear for the investors in this case as they still have an opportunity to convert to *common* shares)

• **Anti-dilution**: protects the investor from new shares being issued at a lower price (a *down round*) by requiring that in that circumstance, additional shares be issued to the investor; **full-ratchet** protection, it's most extreme form, preserves the investor's ownership percentage

• **Redemption right**: allows the investor to reclaim their funds (considered dangerous for *founders*)

- **No shop clause**: prohibits the *founder* from entering into negotiations with other investors (but not necessarily from continuing existing negotiations) for a fixed time period during *due diligence*; the investor will be under no such constraint
- **Voting rights**: (of *preferred stock*, possibly at a multiple of *common*)

Example sentences:

The term sheet was presented to them last night at 8:00 p.m.

The founding team was so intimidated by the complexity of the term sheet that they didn't know where to start negotiating.

She was really surprised when she saw the term sheet, as the valuation was much lower than she had expected.

Quotes:

"For some time Jason and I have felt that VC's have had an unfair advantage when it comes to understanding term sheets." — Brad Feld, Managing Director, Foundry Group

"You'll get a lot more soft offers than firm ones, and more What If offers than signed, binding term sheets. Just because a CEO or SVP at an acquirer talks to you about acquiring you, doesn't mean it will really happen." — Jason M. Lemkin, Managing Director, Storm Ventures

"In all cases, the one fundamental requirement is that the company and the investor agree on how much is being invested, and on what terms. These items are included in what is known as a term sheet." — David S. Rose, Managing Partner, Rose Tech Ventures

"Fundraising is a dangerous time suck for early stage startups ... Realistically you'll need 50 meetings to get interest from 5 investors, which will result in 1 term sheet." — Jon Yongfook Cockle, CEO, Twenty Four Twelve Systems

Capitalization Table

The **capitalization table** (also called the **cap table** or **cap sheet**) represents the details of the *startup*'s ownership and financings. Generally written in a spreadsheet or table format, the cap sheet provides not only a significant record for the *startup* but also a bird's-eye view of the financial standing of the company and its investors.

The capitalization table includes a row for each *class of stock*. For each row, it holds at least the investment amount, *pre and/or post-money valuations*, and the resulting ownership percentage of that and each prior class of stock. A class of stock will exist for each *investment round*, but the cap table can easily be broken down further to show the impact of each *investment round* on individual shareholders.

Liquidation preferences and other terms may separate the ownership percentages on the cap table from the actual payouts upon different *liquidity events*. A **waterfall analysis**, including **liquidation preference charts** (also known as **liquidation curves**), helps express those potential outcomes in terms of the effect of different *exit values* on each shareholder. The name refers to how the remaining *value* cascades through the various *classes of stock* as *preferences* are taken. The cap table is essential to understanding the *dilution* implications of decisions by *startups*, bankers, *venture capitalists*, and other investors regarding further financing or *equity* distribution to employees and their respective terms.

Although the reduction in the *founding team's* ownership percentage as the cap table grows may seem depressing, the cap table should also reveal the increasing worth of those shares.

Example sentences:

She avoided equity crowdfunding for fear of generating an excessively long cap table.

He forgot to bring the cap table, so the meeting was a dud.

They worked on the cap table before deciding to increase the number of stock options for employees.

Quotes:

"Having spent the past 15 years trying to come up with the definitive spread-sheet model for all cases, we've given up. It's really hard to create the general case and actually using it is very difficult. So we don't have a generic cap table to offer." — Brad Feld, Managing Partner, Foundry Group

"But venture capital firms often consider more than just the shares issued to founders and previous investors. They will often also include, in the capi-talization table, the employee stock pool and any outstanding warrants. This is what is referred to as the fully diluted post-money capitalization." — Alexander J. Davie, Attorney, Riggs Davie PLC

"Many entrepreneurs think their pre-money valuation determines their percentage ownership of the company. They forget about the option pool shuffle. They forget about seed debt and its discount. Then they blame their lawyers. They need to understand the cap table." — Babak Nivi, Founder, AngelList

Stock Options

Stock options have become an integral component of employee compensation in *startups*. Common wisdom dictates that employees who have chosen to work in a riskier situation than a more established company should participate in the financial success of the company. Moreover, this incentive can compensate for a *startup's* difficulty in paying salaries and benefits at market rates.

An **employee stock option** (**ESO**)represents a right to buy the underlying stock for some time into the future (the **duration**), often up to 10 years, at a predetermined acquisition price (the **strike price**, or **exercise price**). The objective is for the strike price to represent a substantial discount on the stock's market price at the time of purchase, with the employee benefitting in proportion to that discount. When the strike price exceeds the market price, the option is said to be **underwater**; such options are rarely exercised, for obvious reason. As with a direct grant of *equity*, stock options have significance based on the percentage of ownership potentially transferred. Employee stock options are subject to *vesting* and cannot be exercised until they *vest*.

Of the two types of stock options that a *startup* might grant, **incentive stock options** (**ISOs**) are the more avidly coveted. For ISOs there is normally no ordinary taxable income upon either grant or exercise—only capital gains. **Non-qualified stock option***s* (**NSOs**) are subject to ordinary income tax on the difference between the exercise price and the value of the stock when the option is exercised. ISOs are highly restricted and for employees only, while NSOs may be granted to employees, consultants, and non-employee directors.

Example sentences:

Her stock option package represented a 2% stake in the firm.

She fears that stock option (versus stock) grants encourage risky behavior because the holder participates in upward but not downward movement of the share price.

Given the company's poor performance, his stock options are likely to be worthless.

Quotes:

"HP really did hand out stock options to all of its employees as far back as the late 1940s ... When stock compensation wasn't considered an expense but a high-risk incentive and performance reward, the Valley was braver, more innovative and more dynamic." — Michael S. Malone, Veteran Silicon Valley Historian

"We give out stock options. I hope they're worth money to you some day. But let them be 'icing on the cake'. If they pay off handsomely that's great. But don't count on it." — Mark Suster, Partner, Upfront Ventures

"You should offer stock options wherever possible. I feel strongly that options are important because they incentivize people so that they'll know it's not just a job and that they're really in this family that's trying to build something of value." — Gil Elbaz, Founder & CEO, Factual

"All too often, people don't read statements about how their options work—whether because the explanations seem opaque or there simply aren't enough hours in the day to squeeze in another chore. And that can lead to big problems, because options come with many complex rules attached—and ignoring them can have serious consequences for people's portfolios. People can end up facing substantial tax hits, taking on unnecessary risk or even losing the right to exercise the options entirely." — Veronica Dagher, Wealth Reporter, *The Wall Street Journal*

Portfolio

The **portfolio** refers to the combination (or pool) of companies in which the *VC firm* has invested its *limited partners'* money and those companies are referred to as **portfolio companies**, regardless of which *fund* the investments are part of. A *VC's* holding period for the companies in its portfolio will generally depend on the lifetime of the *fund*.

VCs may provide advice or support (wanted or not) to their portfolio companies, beyond their financial investment. Some of this may be provided by an **entrepreneur-in-residence** (**EIR**). Often, *VCs* find new investments through contacts in their portfolio companies.

Most *VC firms* will specialize in a particular stage of growth. Many specialize in a particular geographic area. Some *VCs* may specialize in a particular industry, while others diversify across industries. In either case, *VCs* will seek an appropriate balance in new investments, hitting their area of interest but avoiding excessive overlap with companies already in their portfolio.

VC firms take seriously the importance of maintaining **deal flow**, i.e., a steady stream of appropriate investments. While this is not a challenge for the most selective, **top-tier** *VCs*, for others it may be difficult.

Of course, the strategy for assembling a portfolio of companies often comes down to a nuanced *valuation* approach. With such high failure rates among *startups*, the winners in the portfolio need to produce outsized returns to offset the damages wreaked by failed companies. Such returns may be reaped at an *exit* event, such as an *IPO* or an *acquisition*. A risky game indeed.

Example sentences:

They have some killer names in their portfolio.

You can look at the VC's website to see the names of their portfolio companies.

They tend to have only bio-tech firms in their portfolio.

Quotes:

"There are three key activities in venture investing: Deciding which start-up(s) to invest in, how much to invest, and how to construct the portfolio." — Matt Oguz, Managing Director, venture/science

"Yes, sometimes these are generalities about how we back talented entrepreneurs building great companies, but taking a look at a VC's portfolio can tell you a lot about the types of companies in which they invest." — Lee Hower, Co-founder, NextView Ventures

"With uncertainty around the financing and exit markets and macro concerns, some VCs are working hard to prepare their portfolio companies and themselves for leaner times." — Anand Sanwal, Co-founder & CEO, CB Insights

"VC firms love to talk about how important they are to their portfolio companies' success. We don't believe in singing our own praises." — Manu Kumar, Founder, K-9 Ventures

"If investors get any signals of trouble, they may pull back on their entire portfolio. Any negative thinking about unicorns can turn into concerns about your entire investment." — Michael Tchong, Founder, Social Revolution

Syndicate

Financings come together for venture backing in numerous ways. Sometimes only one *VC* backs the deal, but if two or more entities invest in it, they form a **syndicate**. A single *VC* (the **lead investor**) may form a syndicate with *angel investors*, other *VCs*, or even *seed-stage funds*, and they jointly provide the capital. Usually all investors get the same *terms*, but occasionally sweeter terms are bestowed on one or another via a **side letter**.

Especially at the *seed round* when the *startup's* risk of failure is greatest, syndicates can serve as a way of reducing that risk through diversification while giving the *startup* access to a greater amount of funding than any one investor alone is willing to provide. In subsequent rounds, issues of diversification and pooling of funds may still be at play. Furthermore, an investor from a prior round may wish to continue to participate and, indeed, it can look very bad for the *startup* if no previous-round investor chooses to carry on (a prospect known as **signaling risk**). Once a *startup* has achieved serious momentum, however, any number of investors may want a piece of the action.

There are also drawbacks to syndication for a *startup*. One partner backing out during negotiations would send a negative signal that could influence others. The smaller percentage ownership granted to each of multiple *VCs* could have adverse consequences such as crowding out new investors if things go very well or making it more likely existing ones will lose interest otherwise. Then there's the unpleasant prospect of in-fighting among syndicated investors.

AngelList has introduced a notion of syndicates among individual investors, where a lead investor entices **backers** to place funds under his or her management. This blurs the lines between *angel investors, venture capitalists,* and *limited partners* (although backers generally must approve each transaction and can leave at any time).

Example sentences:

The seed-round syndicate includes a VC and a bunch of angels.

I heard the lead VC in the syndicate dropped out of the Series A negotiations.

I wish I had gotten into that syndicate.

Quotes:

"Often VCs ask if you want to do a syndicate. Typically this is code that really means 'Instead of selling 25% of the company for $5M, why don't you sell 25% of the company to *each* of us, for $5M and 50% total dilution.'" — Elad Gil, Co-founder, Color Genomics

"And while we've seen an increasing amount of information and transparency about the players in this market, it can be challenging to embark on a set of initial meetings with investors without an understanding of how these VC syndicates are formed." — David Beisel, Co-founder & Partner, NextView Ventures

"I've seen some recent financings where there were six or more [VC firms] in the syndicate." — Fred Wilson, Co-founder, Union Square Ventures

"VC deal syndication is a pretty funny dance, with the entrepreneur trying to get VCs to converge, and venture capitalists trying to feel out each other and the company to see how/where/when an investment might come together. Given the added complexity of getting two VCs at once, many entrepreneurs consider raising capital from a single fund and screwing the whole 'syndication' thing." — Healy Jones, Head of Lead Acquisition, Sunrun

"I make everyone sign a side letter that says I can follow on, I'm pro rata for life. I won't screw with their documents or their deals, but I don't want to get pushed out by a VC who comes in and says they're taking all of it." — Josh Maher, Angel Investor and Author, *Startup Wealth*

Burn Rate

The **burn rate** of a *startup* refers to its negative cash flow—the amount by which its cash expenditures exceed the cash it takes in. This burning of cash typically goes along with starting a company and getting an idea off the ground ... or not. The burn rate is usually calculated as a monthly figure and provides an important indicator to management of how much time they have before they must either raise or earn more money, or close their doors. A *startup* that runs short on cash may also be able to arrange a **bridge note** (a short-term form of *convertible note*) from their *VC*, but it's never good to be desperate.

In a project management context, burn rate refers to net cash expenditures on a project relative to its budget. Rent, salaries, consultants, professional services such as attorneys and accountants, and conference attendance all contribute to the burn rate. The ultimate driver of costs is usually headcount.

The term "burn rate" was made legendary by the dot.com bust of 2000 and came to be associated with the epic amounts of funding that companies were receiving—and burning—prior to going public. During that era, some investors mistakenly perceived the burn rate to be a proxy for how fast the *startup* was acquiring a customer base.

Startups need to *scale*, and *scaling* requires spending. But as Fred Brooks made clear long ago in *The Mythical Man-Month*, you can't always solve a problem faster by throwing more people (thus money) at it. Every *startup* must decide up to what point it is getting its money's worth in a holistic way that recognizes both the bottlenecks strewn throughout the organization and the need for sustainability with respect to expected cash inflows. Bessemer Venture Partners' Byron Deeter breaks these down as: 1) Keeping the company structurally sound for the long term; and 2) Maintaining favorable unit economics.

Example sentences:

How much money are you burning in a month?

She did not want to invest in a company with such a high burn rate.

Because he believes that he can raise more money quickly, he's not so concerned with his firm's high burn rate.

Quotes:

"A good rule of thumb is multiply the number of people on the team by $10k to get the monthly burn. ... That is the 'fully burdened' cost of a person including rent and other costs." — Fred Wilson, Managing Partner, Union Square Ventures

"Your value creation must be at least 3x the amount of cash you're burning, or you're wasting investor value." — Mark Suster, Partner, Upfront Ventures

"The ... unicorns, are heading for a fall every bit as dramatic as their hapless dot-com brethren 15 years ago. The culprit will be exactly the same, their burn rates." — Adam Lashinsky, Asst. Managing Editor, *Fortune*

"Only by evaluating a company's use of cash and long-term strategy can high burn be diagnosed as good or bad. In many cases, the low burn ideal is actually dangerous. At Founders Fund we avoid investing in companies unless they are consuming cash." — Scott Nolan, Partner, Founders Fund

"It doesn't matter whether a company's burn rate is $10K per month or $10 million per month, companies die when their burn rates are greater than investor enthusiasm." — Eric Paley, Managing Partner, Founder Collective

"You need to see if metrics are being met, exceeded (in a bad way, like doubling your burn rate) or totally blown out of the water (in a good way, think doubling your customer sign ups)." — Ja-Nae Duane, Author, *The Startup Equation*

Tranche

When a *startup* raises a *round of funding*, it often collects the funds not all at once but rather on a time schedule where additional funds are released only if certain **milestones** are reached. Those milestones may take the form of sales, user counts, entrance into new markets, or release of product features. French for "slices" or "portions," **tranches** are defined as the individual payments of invested funds.

A *startup* is likely to prefer *investment rounds* without tranches for the same reasons it might prefer long rounds to short ones; this lets them concentrate on their work without distractions, enables them to commit to investments that will grow the firm, and creates a unity of interests between *founders* and investors. Investors, however, may see it differently, desiring a way to limit their downside if the expectations upon which the investment is made are not realized, while locking in a right to double down if they are. Because *startup founders* are optimists, long rounds have the corresponding disadvantage *vis a vis* short ones of selling more of the company at a lower price; if that lower price is to be locked in, a round without tranches is clearly more desirable than one with them, giving up the afore-mentioned benefits.

Startups may therefore be left with a trade-off between raising money through more *investment rounds* or through fewer *rounds* with more tranches in each. Because terms are renegotiated between *investment rounds* but set in advance for tranches, *founders* may consider that since they will be cut off upon missing milestones, they might as well reap the benefit of better terms upon achieving them.

Perhaps tranches could be set with the price increasing along with the expected *value* of the firm. Regardless, tranched investments carry many disadvantages, mostly related to milestone selection, which may be arbitrary or ambiguous and risks locking the *startup* into plans that cease to be advantageous (the opposite of an *Agile* approach).

Example sentences:

The VC was glad to have insisted upon tranches after their MVP was a bust.

Having met their milestone, the startup unlocked the next tranche.

She refuses to accept funding if tranches are involved.

Quotes:

"Just how flawed, for example, can a minimally viable product be and still be said to satisfy a milestone, such as 'release the company's first product to the market'?" — Paul Jones, Co-Chair, Venture Capital Group, Michael Best & Friedrich, LLP

"Don't set yourself up for the impossible by asking for too much—first prove that you can manage your debt or equity capital. Tranche your requests ..." — Joseph Lizio, Founder, Business Money Today

"The idea behind tranching is right, which is to limit the capital at risk (and the dilution) until the business increases in value and risk is mitigated. The right way to do this is [to] raise smaller rounds more frequently and negotiate the prices of each financing as the round is done." — Bill Clark, CEO, MicroAngel Capital Partners

"Investments, like the ocean, can come in waves, but that doesn't mean they should." — Carlos Eduardo Espinal, Partner, SeedCamp

"In theory, tranching gives the VC's a way to mitigate risk and the entrepreneur the comfort of not having to do a roadshow for the next round of financing. In practice, I've found tranching to be a really bad idea." — Chris Dixon, Partner, Andreessen Horowitz

Down Round

A **down round** is a round of financing in which investors purchase stock from the company at a *valuation* lower than that of the previous round.

Down rounds result in **dilution** of ownership for existing shareholders, who retain a reduced percentage of *equity*. Dilution occurs any time a new stockholder purchases shares or one current stockholder purchases more shares than others, but in those common situations the current stockholders retain a smaller piece of a larger pie. In a down round, though, the pie is being recognized as smaller than the current stockholders had thought.

Since previous investors generally have *anti-dilution* clauses, which restore their allocation percentage after a new round that dilutes in this way, the *founding team's* portion of *equity* takes the re-balancing hit. As a result, the *founding team* may find their interest in the company greatly devalued, or even potentially worthless.

While no company wants to raise a down round, it can happen when *valuations* of the company at previous *investment rounds* seem too high at the time of a subsequent round. New investors aren't willing to come in at the previous *valuation* and insist upon a lower price. Examples of why this may occur include the initial *valuation* having been too high, the *startup* failing to meet expectations in the expected time frame between rounds, the *startup* having too high a *burn rate* for the amount of traction it is gaining so that it runs short of cash and is unable to hold out for a higher *valuation*, or a red-hot economy turning bad, causing overall re-evaluation of all *valuations*.

Although they create complications for both past and future investors, and are extremely demoralizing, down rounds can bring in the cash needed to give a company time to turn itself around.

Example sentences:

That down round left the co-founders' and employees' stock options so diluted that they all became disillusioned.

Commentators predicted that the company was set for a down round after such a high valuation.

When the product launch was delayed, the investors were glad to have insisted upon protective provisions against down rounds.

Quotes:

"Talking about down rounds in a bull market feels like shopping for an umbrella in this unprecedented California drought. You get some funny looks, but it pays to be prepared." — Alexander Niehenke, Principal, Scale Venture Partners

"After a few years of massive hype in the startup sector, absurd-sounding valuations are starting to correct themselves. Startups are confronting the prospect of raising 'down rounds' from investors ..." — Alyson Shontell, Deputy Editor, *Business Insider*

"So why is a startup broken after a down round? Well, the entrepreneurs, depending on the type of anti-dilution provisions, are often so diluted that they no longer have a meaningful stake in the startup, and are better off leaving." — David Cummings, Founder & Chairman, Hannon Hill Corporation

"First, a down round sends a signal that something is wrong with your company. Something didn't go to plan. And no amount of explanations 'we raised in a frothy market ...' [will] erase the 'something is wrong' psychology." — Mark Suster, Partner, Upfront Ventures

Exit Strategy

Intrinsically embedded in the concept of a *venture-backed* entity is the end goal of cashing out of the business in what is known as an **exit**. The startup may have as its goal either an *IPO* or an acquisition (buyout) of the firm. The latter form of transaction is serviced by professionals in a sector known as **mergers and acquisitions** (**M&A**). The **exit strategy** refers to the *startup*'s plan for how it wishes to exit. An unfortunate form of exit is the **liquidation** of the company, which can be triggered by the *VC's* need to return funds to its *limited partners*.

The exit event is historically the only way for co-*founders* or *VCs* to cash out on their investment, as they are holding shares that are not publicly traded and as a result have been difficult to sell. Other **liquidity events** are, however, possible. One party may arrange to cash out, in whole or in part, as new money is invested or *startup* shares may be sold on newly arisen and controversial secondary markets. It is possible, but unusual, for the *founding team* and other investors to allow a VC to exit via a **leveraged buyout** (**LBO**), in which the firm becomes collateral for a loan used to compensate the exiting party. The root "liquid" here generally refers to the assets invested in the company becoming available to flow into other ventures, but one should be careful as there may be some ambiguity in who or what is becoming liquid.

The **exit value** is the monetary *value* that the company has, or expects to have, at the time of sale or *IPO*. It will vary depending on external economic conditions, which might favor *IPOs* or M&A. *IPOs* typically yield the highest return on investment, but many companies are happy to be acquired for a generally lower exit value, as the odds of a *startup* reaching an *IPO* are slim.

While *founders* may be unsure how they would exit, it is important to consider because differences with investors on this point can become the basis for conflict down the road.

Example sentences:

For many startups, their exit strategy is to be acquired by Google or Facebook.

The VC and entrepreneur had a falling out over differences in their respective exit strategy preferences.

The founding team was extremely happy with their exit valuation.

Quotes:

"In Silicon Valley, where startup activity is at an unparalleled high, mergers and acquisitions are the fastest-growing exit for venture-backed companies."
— Christina Farr, Digital Health Editor & NPR Contributor, KQED

"Every company needs an exit strategy. Ideally, the exit strategy should be signed off by the founders before the first dollar of external investment goes into the company." — Basil Peters, Author, *Early Exits*

"The more sophisticated plans and pitches will mention recent exits and offer information about how the companies that exited were valued when they were bought. That usually ends up as something like '[this similar company] was purchased by [that company] in [that year] for [that amount], which was [that multiple] of its revenues.' The standard phrase in that context is '5X' for an exit value of five times revenues, or '10X,' or whatever." — Tim Berry, Founder & Chairman, Palo Alto Software

"Most startups fit into a predictable framework when it comes to planning an exit strategy. Emerging companies receive funding from an outside investor at some point. This means that an exit or liquidity event is expected in the not too distant future. Traditional venture capital funds have a lifespan of 10 years. Hence, as the fund reaches maturity, the pressure will mount on the startup CEO to find an exit for the company." — Michel Courtoy, COO, Rozo Systems

IPO

In an **initial public offering** (**IPO**), a company lists its shares on a stock exchange for the first time, providing the public the opportunity to invest in the company's *equity* and growth in the form of publicly traded stock. From this point forward, institutional and individual investors will generally not interact directly with the company to invest capital but will instead buy and sell shares of the company via the stock market.

IPOs are often discounted so that the stock price will shoot up on the first trading day (the first-day "**pop**"), making them a sought-after investment. IPOs, however, are not always sure-fire wins. In some situations, IPO stock has actually lost money from the opening trade price to the closing price of the first day.

Not that long ago in Silicon Valley (and other hot markets), *startups* rushed to get their companies to an IPO. This was considered to be the best *exit* result and a validation of the company's success. More recently, the trend has been to push the IPO out, in some cases to avoid the costs, disclosures, and compliance responsibilities involved with public companies. Furthermore, the burgeoning trend of large companies purchasing promising *startups* as a source of innovation can provide an alternative *exit strategy*. Finally, the still immature—but growing—secondary market for private shares allows employees of private companies a way to cash out, limiting a source of pressure to go to IPO. Nontraditional investors like hedge funds and mutual funds move in, easing the need for an IPO. The resulting pressure on valuations, however, can limit future funding options for the *startup*.

The trend of forestalling IPOs may eventually recede, with some, such as author and investor Andy Kessler, warning that without the discipline of the public market, sky-high *valuations* can become detached from reality.

Example sentences:

Because the IPO was underpriced, demand greatly exceeded supply for the shares offered.

Initially gratified to be included in the IPO, the investor was disappointed with the first-day performance.

Alibaba's $25 billion IPO set a new record for driven entrepreneurs to try to beat.

Quotes:

"[SolarCity's IPO] has not unleashed the flood of clean-tech IPOs that market participants expected in 2013." — Kathy Smith, Principal, Renaissance Capital

"The IPO process and our business then entered a sort of limbo as we waited for, and then responded to, the SEC's comments on our registration statement." — Eric Schmidt, Executive Chairman, Alphabet

"Twenty years ago, IPOs had gotten democratized. You had Microsoft able to go public at less than $1 billion valuation. If you invested in Microsoft's IPO and held you had the prospect in the public market of a 1,000-times gain." — Marc Andreessen, Co-founder, Andreessen Horowitz

"It's nice to do an IPO where your investors get value straightaway and the share price pops up; it proves you left something on the table for them." — Ivan Glasenberg, CEO, Glencore

"We will never sell or have an IPO. What that does is suddenly flushes you with cash. It makes you now work for a group of stockholders, who, again, put pressure and temptations on your true-blueness." — Joel Salatin, Farmer, Polyface

TECHNOLOGY TRENDS

Gamification

Napoleon Bonaparte once said "A soldier will fight long and hard for a bit of colored ribbon." Today, companies are hoping that employees will work long and hard to get "badges" and other electronic equivalents of that bit of ribbon. The vehicle for doing this, called **gamification**, can be applied to affect the behavior not only of employees, but also of customers, students, and practically anybody else an organization comes in contact with.

It is said that motivation has four ingredients: having a clear goal or objective, knowing your progress toward that goal (your score), having control over the outcome, and getting rewarded for meeting your goal (preferably as quickly as possible). The effective combination of these elements is what makes video games so addictive, and indeed game designers carefully plan their games so that the balance and timing of challenge and reward draws in the player and holds their interest.

In gamification, game-like elements such as challenges, points, leaderboards, and levels are adapted for use by employees in the workplace, or by customers as part of their interaction with the company's offering. To apply gamification, a company will identify the behaviors they wish to reward (increased sales, healthy life habits, etc.), choose what rewards they can provide (at the level of resources, emotions, status, etc.), and design a system for granting those rewards. Rewards create a sense of competition, intended to enhance performance and *engagement*. Gamification has been used to promote employee wellness, customer loyalty, and goal achievement.

Gamification raises the question, however, of whether or not it is ethical to manipulate people, even to have them unwittingly act in their own interest.

Example sentences:

My office is applying gamification to the training process to engage employees and improve performance.

The product's use of gamification was so subtle that users didn't realize how much they were spending.

The startup banked on its app's use of gamification to increase user check-ins at its customer's store locations.

Quotes:

"Our point of view on gamification is it all comes down to this idea of motivating people through data. Smart companies can take that data and use that to motivate better performance." — Rajat Paharia, Co-founder & CPO, Bunchball

"It may seem as though gamifying is all about adding various quantities (levels, badges, progress bars) to actions and creating airs of mystery. It may also seem that users are sheep who follow every system like this with more significance than they actually have. The truth is—for the vast majority of users—that if users can't see a point behind the number then they will soon drift away." — Tadhg Kelly, Author, *What Games Are*

"Gamification is design that places the most emphasis on the human in the process. In essence, it is human-focused design." — Yu Kai Chou, Founder & Chief, Octalysis Group

"I think there is a real possibility that companies will look at so-called gamification as a kind of soma for workers. Redesign jobs and mundane tasks so that they are more gamelike, and squeeze ever more productivity out of employees." — Adam Penenberg, Associate Professor, Journalism, New York University

MOOC

A **massive open online course** (**MOOC**) allows open access, via the Internet, to an unlimited number of participants around the world. Some of the first successful MOOCs were Andrew Ng's class on *machine learning* and Sebastian Thrun and Peter Norvig's class on *artificial intelligence* in 2011. MOOCs became widespread by 2012 (which the *New York Times* called "The year of the MOOC"), propelled by startups that Ng and Thrun were involved in founding.

MOOCs provide instruction and problem sets suitable for **distance learning**. Many also provide forums that support interaction between students, professors, and teaching assistants. MOOCs have the potential to engage students and customize education to their individual styles and needs in a way not possible in traditional lectures.

Despite the benefits and ease that MOOCs offer, they have many detractors. Some argue that website lectures cannot replace the unique experience of sitting in a classroom. The quality of MOOCs often varies dramatically. And some have noted the low completion rates of many MOOCs. Although many MOOCs are free, some charge for their services. Organizers have found that charging a fee increases student commitment—and thus completion rates. Free MOOCs may be financed by corporate sponsors.

Contrasting with MOOCs are **SPOC**s. A SPOC is a **small private online course**. It is often aimed at on-campus students. As with MOOCs, students using SPOCs work at their own pace and learn interactively through online lectures and labs.

Appropriate roles for traditional universities and technological solutions are being discussed and experimented with throughout Silicon Valley, but it seems uncontroversial that improved access to lifetime learning is essential.

Example sentences:

I heard that someone living in Africa was able to get an MBA's worth of classes through MOOCs offered by major American universities.

MOOCs allow a single parent to get an education while working.

The startup was making it easy for anybody to create a MOOC.

Quotes:

"MOOC is the new textbook." — David Finegold, Chief Academic Officer, American Honors

"I feel strongly that degrees are really valuable to people, and having MOOCs allow for credit down the line will increase the number of students with the confidence and wherewithal to complete degrees." — Daphne Koller, Co-founder & President, Coursera

"There is a dire need for some healthy skepticism among educators about the idea that MOOCs are a wonderful means to go global in order to do good." — Ghanashyam Sharma, Assistant Professor, Writing and Rhetoric, State University of New York at Stony Brook

"Far from realizing the high ideals of their advocates, MOOCs seem to be reinforcing the advantages of the 'haves' rather than educating the 'have nots.'" — Ezekiel Emanuel, Chair, Department of Medical Ethics and Health Policy, University of Pennsylvania

"Whether or not SPOCs amount to some sort of pedagogical revolution, it seems clear that they hold more promise than pure MOOCs when it comes to delivering students a full educational experience—not to mention saving academics' jobs." — Will Oremus, Senior Technology Writer, *Slate*

Sharing Economy

The **sharing economy** is an expanding *business model* built on the idea of **collaborative consumption**, i.e., people relying on each other in obtaining access to merchandise. The core of the model is the *consumer* renting underused assets from other *consumers*, rather than purchasing new ones. First identified in the mid-2000s, it was galvanized by the radical expansion of social media, the development of the mobile Internet, and a growing sense of urgency regarding natural resource depletion.

This community practice has transformed into a very profitable *business model* for those running such **online marketplaces**, and in some cases for the "sellers." These brokers, utilizing both the Internet and mobile apps, have increased efficiency, reduced transaction costs, and made it possible for anyone to advertise their property and services. Prominent players include Airbnb (renting your home), RelayRides (renting your car), JustPark (renting your parking space), DogVacay (housing people's pets while they are on vacation), and Lyft and Uber (driving your car for others).

As these latter examples indicate, the sharing economy tends to blur into the *gig economy*, whereby people are enabled via web sites or mobile apps to work as contractors in place of steady employment.

Traditional competitors have raised concerns that such companies have an unfair advantage because they often do not comply with regulations that protect the public—and themselves, to varying degrees; in many cases legacy firms have challenged sharing economy firms in court. It appears likely, however, that the sharing economy is here to stay.

Example sentences:

Although it seemed that all the low-hanging fruit was taken, the *startup* thought it had a new angle on the sharing economy.

At first, I made a fortune driving my car in the sharing economy, but now everybody's doing it.

What do you think is the next frontier in the sharing economy?

Quotes:

"I'd like to talk about a movement for the sharing economy. By 'a movement' I mean exactly that. I mean huge numbers of people with a shared identity, mobilized to take actions to... grow the peer sharing economy, and to fight for their collective interests." — Douglas Atkins, Director of Community, Airbnb

"The growing sharing economy is leveraging technology and innovation to generate new jobs and income for San Franciscans in every neighborhood and at every income level." — Ed Lee, Mayor, San Francisco

"I'm going to ... try and convince you that [collaborative consumption] isn't a flimsy idea, or a short-term trend, but a powerful cultural and economic force reinventing not just what we consume, but how we consume." — Rachel Botsman, Co-Author, *What's Mine is Yours*

"Many Americans are making extra money renting out a small room, designing websites, selling products they design themselves at home or even driving their own car. This on-demand, or so-called gig economy is creating exciting economies and unleashing innovation. But it is also raising hard questions about work-place protections and what a good job will look like in the future." — Hillary Clinton, 2016 Presidential Candidate

SoLoMo (Social-Local-Mobile)

SoLoMo, a portmanteau of **Social-Local-Mobile**, represents a model for connecting mobile users with local commerce based on their location and social media activity. The growing popularity of the smartphone influenced and allowed for the emergence of this trend. Unlike the PC, which can be located only by its IP address, the smartphone can be tracked by more precise GPS coordinates that are exchanged with applications. Furthermore, these apps make mobile phone users' social media activities and interests available for analysis that can yield further location validation and a more personalized experience. This combination of technologies provides access to the huge market of small local businesses that is difficult to reach by other means. From the perspective of local businesses, it finally lets them stand out to ever-more-connected users where they have the strongest competitive advantage—literally in their own backyard.

Search engines have acknowledged the significance of the shift in search technology. By employing **geolocation** and social media history, many search engines now tap into the previously untouched local market, presenting local businesses over more generic options. It's been estimated that 80% of mobile users prefer localized search results, and 75% of users are more likely to take action if a local option is presented.

The emergence of SoLoMo represents a complete *paradigm shift* from the tradition of publishing standard messages to all users. Instead, relevant *content* leveraging local offerings is presented by determining a user's location and activity on social media. Forrester analyst Jenny Wise argues that the SoLoMo vision is too limited, and that what is really needed is to analyze a person's entire context and to access them at whatever device they happen to be using. Applications should be built from the ground up following these principles in order to obtain higher levels of *user engagement*.

Example sentences:

With our SoLoMo app, you can invite a friend who is nearby to join you shopping to help you pick out clothes.

After three years working for Groupon, she'd had enough of SoLoMo.

SoLoMo seemed like a new idea to them just a few years ago, but now it's totally baked into their business strategy.

Quotes:

"The next generation of leaders and start-ups to emerge will involve mobile, local and social." — Eric Schmidt, Executive Chairman, Alphabet

"Whether it's for a small coffee shop or a large retailer, SoLoMo works equally well for small and large businesses." — Joseph Ruiz, President, Strategic Marketing Solutions

"Social, Mobile, and Local represent modes of ubiquity, which is to say they are ways of accessing individuals wherever they are, and these work best when integrated such that the end user has a continuous experience of your business/brand." — Jordan Baines, VP, Strategy & Analytics, Accomplice VC

"We thought what we should really do is try to put an inclusive concept around these three megatrends that seem to be driving a lot of new value, and point out that it is at the integration of these three megatrends that a lot of products and services are being created." — Chi-Hua Chien, Co-founder & Managing Partner, Goodwater Capital

"The 'social, mobile, local' and 'Uber of Everything' movement that has dominated conversation as of late has been, at its core, a fundamentally consumer-focused phenomenon." — Chris Myers, Co-founder & CEO, BodeTree

Big Data

The ubiquity of sensors and decreasing cost of storage have led to an explosion of data. This **big data**, and concomitant leaps in analytic tools and storage technology, create an unprecedented opportunity for applications to provide users with *value*, for companies to better understand their business—and for individuals billing themselves as **data scientists**. One common use of big data, **predictive analytics**, aims to *micro-segment consumers* and predict their behavior. More generally, *machine learning* algorithms react to patterns in data rather than explicit instruction to provide appropriate responses.

Big data has multiple defining characteristics, all chosen, by convention, to start with the letter 'V.' The initial three were proposed in 2001 by META Group analyst Doug Laney. A data set may exhibit one or more of these characteristics to be considered "big data." First, big data has a very large **volume**, meaning that there's a lot of it. It may also have high **velocity**, meaning that it's generated at great speed. John Joseph, then of Lavastorm, notes that **volatility**, emphasizing the speed at which data changes, is a more appropriate trait name. The **variety** of big data can have several interpretations. When data occurs in the form of numerous attributes, it provides both a challenge to determine relevance and an opportunity to benefit from it. Laney's interpretation indicates that data can take many forms. The broadest categorization is between **structured data**, organized by well-defined types (as in a traditional database) and **unstructured data**, usually referring to text. The challenge of data variety comes when data in different formats must be *harmonized*. Many other characteristics of big data have been proposed (and many derided by analytics strategy consultant Seth Grimes as "wanna-V's"). Among these, **veracity**, i.e., that big data may come from untrustworthy sources, was proposed by IBM. **Variance**, the range of possible values, technically folds into volume. **Variability**, seen as how much of the data is subject to change, can be relevant to maintaining consistency.

The biggest challenge of big data is how to use it appropriately and intelligently. Tools that aid in **data visualization** can help with that. But for many people, the greatest concern with the big data accumulating in corporate and government databases is their own privacy. Questions such as "Whose data is it anyway?" must be addressed.

Example sentences:

How can we leverage our big data?

She applied for schooling as a data scientist because given all of the hype surrounding big data, those positions always seemed to be the highest-paying.

People are concerned about the privacy implications of big data.

Quotes:

"The accuracy & nature of answers you get on large data sets can be completely different from what you see on small samples. Big data provides a competitive advantage." — Peter Skomoroch, Data Scientist, Data Wrangling

"Big data used to be called Analytics/Business Intelligence before the industry felt the need for a sexier term." — Balaji Viswanathan, Product Manager, Black Duck

"Big data is worth absolutely nothing without big judgment." — Joseph Bradley, Founder & VP, IoT/IoE Practice, Cisco

"A Data Scientist is a Data Analyst who lives in San Francisco." — Dave Holtz, PhD Candidate in Information Technology, Massachusetts Institute of Technology

Cloud Computing

Cloud computing is the deployment of a network of servers to allow users to upload data and export processing. An **external cloud** involves remote servers, reducing the need to store and process information on local computing devices. These are generally also **public clouds**, in which hardware is allocated among multiple, unrelated **tenants**.

The three primary instantiations of cloud computing export, ordered by decreasing comprehensiveness, software applications (*software as a service, SaaS*), *platforms* to create, run, and manage such applications (**platform as a service, PaaS**), and computing resources (**infrastructure as a service, IaaS**). A recent addition exports analytics processing (**analytics as a service, AaaS**). In any of these cases, processing is said to take place in **the cloud**.

To alleviate security concerns around public clouds, some companies implement **private cloud**s within their corporate firewall. In a **community cloud**, users share computing resources. A **hybrid cloud** combines these mechanisms, allowing more control over local resources, but also affording an opportunity to supplement these with external resources.

Because cloud computing customers pay on an on-demand basis, they avoid upfront infrastructure costs and can economically adjust their use to meet fluctuating needs. Furthermore, cloud services allow companies to outsource much of their IT management work and focus on the projects that differentiate their business. Cloud technologies promote collaboration by ensuring software compatibility and accessibility of data, and make it easier for employees to *work remotely*. The cloud's reach makes possible many new *business models* and, importantly, it has lowered the cost of starting a business, thus promoting *entrepreneurship*.

The next frontier, alluding to a dispersed cloud, is **fog computing**, in which some data and processing are pushed towards the **edge** of a network, occupied by devices, including users' mobile devices, that sense or modify their environment. Such architectures may provide efficiencies deemed essential for *The Internet of Things* and enable enhanced privacy of the localized data.

Example sentences:

My business has been able to divert more funds to marketing since the cloud has reduced infrastructure costs.

Cloud computing allows our employees around the world to share information reliably and in real time.

We are much better able to ride the waves of customer demand with our elastic cloud-based architecture.

Quotes:

"The interesting thing about cloud computing is that we've redefined cloud computing to include everything that we already do." — Larry Ellison, Chairman, Oracle

"The cloud services companies of all sizes … The cloud is for everyone. The cloud is democracy." — Marc Benioff, CEO, Salesforce

"Every kid coming out of Harvard, every kid coming out of school now thinks he can be the next Mark Zuckerberg, and with these new technologies like cloud computing, he actually has a shot." — Marc Andreessen, Co-founder, Andreessen Horowitz

"Cloud computing is based on the time-sharing model we leveraged years ago before we could afford our own computers. The idea is to share computing power among many companies and people, thereby reducing the cost of that computing power to those who leverage it. The value of time share and the core value of cloud computing are pretty much the same, only the resources these days are much better and more cost effective." — David Linthicum, SVP, Cloud Technology Partners

Software As A Service

Software as a service (**SaaS**) is a software distribution model in which a vendor or service provider hosts applications over the Internet and makes them available to customers. Software is centrally hosted and licensed on a subscription basis. This is the most common form of *cloud computing*, whereby the organization's data and much of its processing reside elsewhere.

SaaS relies on underlying technologies such as web services and service oriented architecture (for structuring applications) and asynchronous data transfer (for responsive *user interfaces*), and has benefited from the maturation of those technologies. Centralized hosting of business applications dates back to the 1960s but was interrupted by the PC revolution. The expansion of the Internet in the 1990s supported a new class of centralized computing that eventually developed into SaaS, which now plays a role in office messaging systems, CRM software, payroll processing software, and many other applications.

Software as a service has two *business models*: **hosted application management** and **software on demand.** They differ only in whether the hosting company is also the software developer.

This developing technology presents several benefits. Software as a service supports easier administration, automatic updates and patch management, better compatibility among users, who will be on the same software version, and global accessibility via the web. It also allows the customer more flexibility in deciding what software to use and when.

Although SaaS is likely to remain a primary means of software delivery for some time to come, the more traditional approach of selling a license to download and use software is making a resurgence in the form of an **app economy** for the iPhone and Android mobile *platforms*.

Example sentences:

Before signing with the hosting company for our SaaS delivery, we made sure that we would have the ability to download our data at any time.

We were grateful for having gone with SaaS delivery after deciding to change our software package after only a few months.

Our company decided to deliver its software product on a SaaS model because that is what most customers now prefer.

Quotes:

"Software as a service is about service (not product)." — Chuck DeVita, President, Growth Process Group

"It seems like the web, particularly software as a service, provides ample opportunities for you to flourish economically, completely aligned with the broader open source community." — Matt Mullenweg, Founder & CEO, Automattic Inc.

"There are hundreds of thousands of businesses that have chosen SaaS applications to drive key aspects of their business in some way." — Aaron Rothschild, Director, Product Management, Influitive

"Line-of-business leaders everywhere are bypassing IT departments to get applications from the cloud (also known as software as a service, or SaaS) and paying for them like they would a magazine subscription. And when the service is no longer required, they can cancel that subscription with no equipment left unused in the corner." — Daryl Plummer, Managing VP, Chief of Research, & Chief Gartner Fellow, Gartner

Platform

In broad terms, a **platform** is an underlying computing environment with distinct rules and protocols that other technologies (software, hardware, applications, *cloud computing*, operating systems, etc.) must conform to in order to run properly. A platform can itself be hardware or software. A newer usage of "platform" refers to a web site or mobile app that brings multiple parties together to complete transactions , as in a *multisided business model*. To some, it seems, pretty much any application is a platform.

"Platform" can refer to a single system or a set of layered facilities provided to aid in software development (a **technology stack**). Common components are an operating system, a web server, a database, and a programming language. Platforms can be accessed through *the cloud* via *PaaS*. Cross-platform technology involves the implementation of a common higher-level platform (such as Java bytecode) on multiple lower-level platforms. This allows a developer to reach users of those lower-level platforms while interacting only with the higher-level one (the traditional notion of compilation).

For a technology company, creating a platform is a way to empower users. Rather than predicting what specific problem customers are likely to encounter and providing them with a specific solution, the company can provide a platform to enable an *ecosystem* of developers to compete among themselves to satisfy end-customer needs, all built upon a common solution infrastructure. This gives incredible reach to the technology underlying the platform.

A web browser, for example, can be thought of as a platform that executes web pages defined in HTML, JavaScript, etc., allowing any number of web sites to function. Modern browsers are often platforms in another sense: they can be extended via add-ons. Thus, the organization creating the browser need no longer ensure that every service that every user might desire is present, but only that it is possible for outside developers to create such services.

Example sentences:

This version of the accounting software runs on a different platform than ours.

They want to design their new product for whatever platform has the most users globally.

I don't understand why he sticks with his Blackberry, since almost no apps run on that platform.

Quotes:

"Most software developers ... are perfectly happy just to write software applications. You know programs that do something or solve some particular problem. But the brave among us want to change the world more significantly, and they choose to work on platforms: big giant slabs of software that don't quite do anything out of the box, but which enable a whole world of new and interesting applications." — Joel Spolsky, CEO, Stack Overflow

"Our goal is not to build a platform; it's to be across all of them." — Mark Zuckerberg, CEO, Facebook

"All of these applications and the productivity we've been able to achieve here at Oracle are because of this enormously powerful platform." — Larry Ellison, Chairman, Oracle

"Be scared of platforms ... every trend you could name, I think it's overrated. You should be thinking 'fraud.'" — Peter Thiel, Managing Partner, Founders Fund

"28.2% of the applications for the upcoming YC batch call what they're building a 'platform.'"— Paul Graham, Co-founder, Y Combinator

Internet of Things

The **Internet of Things** (**IoT**) is a scenario in which connected computing devices proliferate and merge with the everyday objects we take for granted. These objects can thus transmit large amounts of information to each other, opening up new possibilities for their intelligent and coordinated operation and potentially limiting the need for human involvement in their maintenance. In other words, physical objects are embedded with sensors and given connectivity so that they become part of a network.

The IoT had been in development since the early 1980s. The first Internet-connected appliance was developed at Carnegie Mellon University—a Coke machine able to report inventory levels and drink temperatures. Since then, the IoT has progressed into **smart grid** (with connected appliances, meters, power generators, and storage cells), *connected vehicles* (to avoid collisions or coordinate with traffic signals), *supply chain* management (monitoring the freshness of merchandise or the conditions that it experienced), medical devices, environmental monitoring, etc. One recent application is a solar-powered garbage can that can announce its remaining capacity to sanitation trucks. The IoT is expected to take *big data* to another level as sensors become more ubiquitous.

While the Internet of Things promises a world in which our every need is anticipated, many have raised criticisms regarding the concept. Privacy concerns over user consent, freedom of choice, and anonymity have been voiced as the system has grown to encompass many diverse fields. Security also poses a serious threat, as the IoT may connect and thus expose more critical systems, making them vulnerable to *hacking*. For these reasons, in addition to the drastically increased number of connected devices that must be handled, an over-haul of the tried-and-true Internet may be called for.

Example sentences:

His sensor management startup was capitalizing on the IoT craze.

The Internet of Things sounds interesting, but I'm not sure I want my toilet to be Internet connected.

She applied to an IoT-focused accelerator program.

Quotes:

"The IoT is big news because it ups the ante: 'Reach out and touch somebody' is becoming 'reach out and touch everything.'" — Parker Trewin, Senior Director of Content and Communications, Aria Systems

"The Internet of things ... will change everything—including ourselves." — Dave Evans, Chief Futurist, Cisco

"The IoT will generate an enormous, truly unprecedented amount of precise information about buyers and their needs. It's a marketer's dream come true." — Jon Gettinger, Senior Vice President, Marketing, Xamarin

"The Internet of Things revolves around increased machine-to-machine communication; it's built on cloud computing and networks of data-gathering sensors; it's mobile, virtual, and instantaneous connection; and they say it's going to make everything in our lives from streetlights to seaports 'smart.'" — Daniel Burrus, Founder & CEO, Burrus Research

"Something often overlooked when we talk about all the shiny new connected gadgets emerging out of the 'Internet of Things' is what happens to all the old things. I'm fascinated by the power of adding multiple sensors to old things and then connecting them to the internet." — Scott Weiss, General Partner, Andreessen Horowitz

Internet of Value

A **cryptocurrency** is a medium of financial exchange playing a similar role to other currencies, but entirely virtual. For purposes of security and anti-counterfeiting, *encryption* techniques are used to regulate the generation of units of currency and the transfer of funds. **Decentralized cryptocurrencies** are not managed by any authority, such as a country's central bank, a feature appealing to civil libertarians.

Developed in 2009 by the mysterious "Satoshi Nakamoto," **Bitcoin** was the first (and remains the best-known) decentralized cryptocurrency. Bitcoins can be generated by running a "**mining**" program that solves complex math problems, producing a **proof of work** with which it is easy to confirm the calculation. The mining process also validates transactions, converting them, along with the proof, to a **block**, which is added to a distributed public ledger called a **block chain**. Inflation is averted by the difficulty of performing the work, rather than the self-control of any government. The Bitcoin software is set to eventually cap the number of Bitcoins in circulation.

It is now recognized that the applications of the block chain's **distributed ledger technology (DLT)** go well beyond currencies. Much as U.S. bills once represented gold, a customized cryptocurrency can stand in for any asset, allowing for a secure and efficient exchange framework, referred to as the **Internet of Value (IoV),** with the potential to *disrupt* firms providing escrow services (e.g., for collectibles and real estate) or ensuring integrity of *supply chains*. **Cryptocontracts** are computer programs that automatically execute the terms of a cryptocurrency-denominated contract.

The proof of a currency's utility is whether it can actually be exchanged for goods and services. Cryptocurrencies have thus far been plagued by extreme volatility and criminal activity. Current cryptocurrencies are limited by the inefficiencies inherent in "mining", the need to distribute the entire block chain, and the lack of a way to manage identities. Low transaction costs and numerous potential applications, however, suggest a bright future for these technologies.

Example sentences:

She knew the Feds wouldn't be able to track her purchase using Bitcoin.

Eventually, his bets on football games will be settled automatically via cryptocontracts.

There is a Bitcoin vending machine at Hacker Dojo in Mountain View, but I've never seen anyone using it.

Quotes:

"Bitcoin is a remarkable cryptographic achievement and the ability to create something that is not duplicable in the digital world has enormous value." — Eric Schmidt, Executive Chairman, Google

"The concept behind the internet of value is that, with new technology, value in the future will move like information has been moving over the last 20 years through the internet." — John Ginovsky, Contributing Editor, *Banking Exchange*

"Bitcoin is an experiment and like all experiments, it can fail. So don't invest what you can't afford to lose." — Mike Hearn, CEO, Vinumeris

"Cryptocurrency is such a powerful concept that it can almost overturn governments" — Charles Lee, Co-founder, LiteCoin

"Silicon Valley is coming. There are hundreds of startups with a lot of brains and money working on various alternatives to traditional banking. ... Competitors are coming in the payments area. You all have read about Bitcoin..." — Jamie Dimon, CEO, JP Morgan

Virtual Reality

Virtual reality (**VR**) replaces sensory data with generated content intended to seem real. This has been a philosophers' dream since Hilary Putnam's "brain in a vat" thought experiment (itself inspired by René Descartes' "evil demon"), and technology is finally catching up.

The term was coined by Jaron Lanier, who did early VR research. A main challenge for the technology is to generate incremental changes to the scene quickly enough in response to a subject's movements that the viewer does not get nauseous. All eyes are on Oculus (whose Rift is the premier VR product), which was initially *crowdfunded*, then *venture-backed*, and eventually purchased by Facebook—all prior to product release. Virtual reality technology tantalizingly promises to bring fantasy to life.

Computer games have often beckoned us to blur the lines between the real and the unreal. **Virtual worlds** go a step further in simulating or recreating real-world features such as people, organizations, and establishments, possibly along-side fictional or historical ones. In a virtual world, multiple "players" can interact via representations called **avatars**. Second Life is the most widely-used virtual world.

Augmented reality, i.e., real-time superimposition on an actual scene of computer-generated information potentially derived from sensors or databases, is a form of **mediated reality**, which more generally changes (adds, modifies, or removes) sensory inputs. It may leverage advances in eyewear such as Google Glass or Microsoft HoloLens to, for example, provide information about people in view using facial recognition technology or enable *consumers* to virtually try on clothes, cosmetics, or haircuts. *Enterprise* applications, which by their nature involve fewer privacy concerns, may come first. While virtual reality may allow student surgeons to perform simulated operations, augmented reality may enhance actual operations by allowing surgeons to visualize what lies beneath the skin.

Example sentences:

The virtual reality startup will support vicarious cliff-diving.

His avatar is pretty scary-looking.

Investors are placing bets on various augmented reality firms.

Quotes:

"[Virtual reality] seeks to fool the user into believing they're someplace else."
— Ben Kuchera, Senior Editor, Opinion, *Polygon*

"[Virtual reality] is very social and it is going to connect people. But right now it looks isolating." — Robert Scoble, Entrepreneur in Residence, UploadVR

"The promise of virtual reality has always been enormous. Put on these goggles, go nowhere, and be transported anywhere. It's the same escapism peddled by drugs, alcohol, sex, and art—throw off the shackles of the mundane through a metaphysical transportation to an altered state."
— Matthew Schnipper, Managing Editor, *Pitchfork*

"I believe that augmented reality will be the biggest technological revolution that happens in our lifetimes ... Once you have an augmented reality display, you don't need any other form of display. Your smart phone does not need a screen. You don't need a tablet. You don't need a TV. You just take the screen with you on your glasses wherever you go." — Tim Sweeney, CEO, Epic Games

"I think I've seen five or six computer demos in my life that made me think the world was about to change: Apple II, Netscape, Google, iPhone ... then Oculus. It was that kind of amazing." — Chris Dixon, Partner, Andreessen Horowitz

Semantic Search

Semantic search is an information-searching technique that goes beyond comparing *keywords* in attempting to determine the intent behind the **search query** entered by the user, so as to generate more relevant results. It may be used for searching within closed dataspaces or on the Internet.

Semantic search is based on **semantics**, the science of meaning of language, and may make use of **natural language processing** (**NLP**) to understand both the search query and the corpus being searched. One challenge here is **word sense disambiguation**, i.e., determining the most probable intended meaning from all possible ones. Conversely, a search related to a given concept should return results without regard to the specific phrasing used. Another challenge is **entity and relationship extraction**, the determination of what real-world people and things are being referenced and how they relate.

Meeting these challenges clearly requires substantial real-world knowledge. A **semantic network** can encode knowledge about the real world (things and relationships and the concepts that can categorize them), and tie that knowledge to language syntax. The **Semantic Web** is intended to be a common repository for such *content*. It may finally come to fruition through the accessibility of **linked data**, i.e., an association of entities with web addresses that could give web pages access to this information. Such a framework is seen as necessary infrastructure for the *Internet of Things* and *cryptocontracts*.

Semantic search may also take into account **user context**—the time and location, the larger set of activities from which the search takes place, the involvement of any other individuals, etc. Search engines are continually being enhanced so as to provide more benefits of semantic search. At the limit here are recommendation engines, in which the query is not supplied by the user at all but instead is derived from their behavior and context.

Example sentences:

With my search engine's new semantic enhancements, I can find what I'm looking for much more easily.

The new semantic search algorithm defeated many SEO tricks.

My startup leverages semantic search to find relevant advice.

Quotes:

"We are at a moment in which semantic search, the ability to put typed searches into context, represents the most accurate option for granting answers." — David Amerland, Author, *Google Semantic Search*

"Semantic search may ultimately be invisible to us as we take on more complex interactions with the 'system.'" — Denise A.D. Bedford, Goodyear Professor of Knowledge Management, Kent State University

"There are small semantic search engines for various verticals already now such as Biotechnology ..., but for semantic search to touch all realms of various domains in different verticals will take longer than anticipated." — Abhishek Shivkumar, Data Scientist, Big Data Partnership

"In the end it is going to be the marriage of Big Data, Semantic Search and User Generated Content that will tell the story of intent for consumers." — Daniel Newman, Co-CEO, V3B

"The robot uses natural language processing to analyse the user's emotional state and respond with appropriate questions, comments and recommendations." — Michelle Avenant, Journalist, *ITWeb*

"The 'semantic web' describes a web where data is understood by computers in some of the same ways humans understand it." — Margaret Heller, Digital Services Librarian, Loyola University Chicago

Artificial Intelligence

Although the search for **artificial intelligence** (**AI**) did not originate in Silicon Valley, it has taken hold here and evokes visions of the *Singularity*. Automation of tasks traditionally requiring human involvement underpins many of the most exciting technologies being developed here today, including voice-activated **virtual assistants**, robotics, and *self-driving* cars. It is easy to make a system seem intelligent if the range of inputs it is expected to consider is tightly constrained (e.g., a chess board). The real challenge of AI is robustness, i.e., systems broadly defined to work across a variety of situations, formalized as **domains**. The quest for **artificial general intelligence** (**AGI**) pushes the minimization of domain assumptions to its limit, aiming for systems that can operate freely in every-day human contexts.

Broadly inspired by a human sense of our proudest accomplishments, **Good Old-fashioned Artificial Intelligence** (**GOFAI**) systems access symbolic representations (models or maps) that extract essential features of some real-world domain. They may use an **ontology** to define characteristics and relationships of the most relevant entities in the domain. Some hope to achieve robustness by **harmonizing** systems created independently for different purposes, translating between their distinct representations, perhaps using an **upper ontology** general enough to describe the common features of entities and their interaction across all domains. Knowledge organized in this way can be made available through the *Semantic Web*.

The more humble, trusting approach of statistical **machine learning** devotes programming effort only to building algorithms that can be **trained** to recognize and predict known patterns or even discover anomalies. Such systems, often implemented on **connectionist** architectures such as **neural networks**, eschew representations in place of direct contact with the environment. One disadvantage is that logical explanations for their recommendations are often unavailable.

Appreciation for the power of the dynamically constructed and statistically derived behaviors of machine learning, and especially the layered approach of **deep learning**, is growing, although the promise of understandable and verifiably correct systems remains appealing. Is it possible to build systems that apply logical reasoning over richly interrelated concepts in a traceable way, ultimately on the basis of machine learning algorithms? Our very existence appears to demonstrate that it is. On the other hand, just as we use language to communicate with each other, semantic representations may remain the best hope of connecting people with computer systems and even computer systems with each other. As in the human case, there is some question of whether a single *lingua franca* is possible or even desirable.

Example sentences:

The anti-GOFAI purist refused to code any representations whatsoever.

When it comes to virtual assistants, I prefer Echo over Siri.

Their startup makes machine-learning algorithms easier to use.

Quotes:

"Artificial intelligence research has foundered on the issue of representation. When intelligence is approached in an incremental manner, with strict reliance on interfacing to the real world through perception and action, reliance on representation disappears." — Rodney Brooks, Founder, Chairman, & CTO, Rethink Robotics

"Artificial Intelligence was born in Computer Science departments, and inherited their value sets including Correctness. This mindset, this necessity to be logical, provable, and correct has been a fatal roadblock for Artificial Intelligence since its inception." — Monica Anderson, CTO, Sensai Corporation

Autonomous Vehicles

Autonomous vehicles, aka **robocars**, are **self-driving**, i.e., they sense their environment and operate without human input. Aerial vehicles can also be autonomous, although **teleoperated** drones (controlled remotely) are not. Self-driving cars were viewed as science fiction only a decade ago, but many automobile manufacturers are now planning them. Autonomous vehicles are an endpoint on a continuum through which the burden on the driver is being reduced.

Self-driving cars may maintain maps and even update them based on sensory input that they gather. Radar, GPS, and **computer vision** are utilized to help the car sense its surroundings. Control systems interpret sensory information to identify roads, obstacles, and signs.

Seemingly opposite technology relates to **connected vehicles**—cars able to communicate with each other (**vehicle-to-vehicle, V2V**) or with stationary facilities such as traffic signals (**vehicle-to-infrastructure, V2I**). It can be used to subordinate driver input to such communications, voluntarily or otherwise—for example, to prevent cars from crossing red lights or to coordinate the distance between vehicles. This technology informs the vision of **intelligent transportation systems** (ITS). The communication can be provided either as **dedicated short-range communication** (DSRC) or through Internet access, perhaps via wireless local area networks relayed between vehicles. **Telematics** systems leverage inter-vehicle communications to provide services including enhanced navigation, in-vehicle entertainment, and vehicle tracking.

While ethical and legal issues abound (such as who's liable for accidents, what values should underlie vehicle *training, cybersecurity* concerns of vehicle *hacking,* and privacy implications of third parties knowing everywhere we travel), it is expected that this technology will save many lives. There is ongoing debate over the extent to which future vehicles will be autonomous or connected, but in one respect these points are not opposed. Whether vehicles act on their own or in conjunction with each other and the roadway, the human driver can be expected to play a diminishing role.

Example sentences:

I can't wait to get a self-driving car so I can take a nap on the way to work during rush hour.

He thinks people won't want to own their robocars, but I disagree.

She developed an app for connected cars at the hackathon.

Quotes:

"We still don't know how autonomous cars will communicate, who'll be liable for failures or how they'll mix with old-fashioned cars." — Des Toups, Managing Editor, *Insurance.com*

"One of my first rules of robocars is 'you don't change the infrastructure.' Changing infrastructure is very hard, very expensive, requires buy-in from all sorts of parties who are slow to make decisions, and even if you do change it, you then have a functionality that only works in the places you have managed to change it." — Brad Templeton, Chair, Networks and Computers, Singularity University

"Meeting the challenge of a transformation to a cleaner and more modern transportation sector requires infrastructure that reduces congestion not by just paving new lanes, but by making better use of the lanes and capacity we have. Autonomous vehicles offer us a realistic way of doing that." — Anthony Foxx, U.S. Secretary of Transportation

Synthetic Biology

Sometimes it seems like practically everybody in Silicon Valley is a software engineer. We are surrounded, however, by devices whose resilience and *scale* exceeds anything that software engineers can direct or control and whose programming languages we are only beginning to appreciate—biological systems.

Synthetic biology applies engineering principles to the fundamental components of biology in order to design and create new life. Its goal is to design biological systems by creating novel artificial biological pathways, organisms, or devices, or by redesigning natural ones. The **CRISPR** technique, derived from a defense system of strep bacteria, has made gene-editing more accessible. These engineered biological systems could be used for purposes such as processing information, manipulating chemicals, fabricating materials and structures, producing energy, consuming environmental toxins, providing food, and maintaining and enhancing health. A holy grail would be to harness photosynthesis from plants to produce energy.

An MIT-based effort is underway to standardize DNA segments in a **parts registry** so that they can be reliably combined to produce predictable results. Such parts can be extracted from simple organisms in which they are well understood or developed using **directed evolution**, which mutates DNA and selects that which produces desired proteins or nucleic acids. Synthetic biology is complicated by **epigenetics**, the influence of environmental factors on behavioral traits through regulation of gene activity, as well as differences in individual genomes.

Although synthetic biology offers extraordinary promise, there are many risks. Manipulating life forms, even with the best intentions, could have unintended consequences; the technology could be weaponized to intentionally inflict harm. Many have ethical concerns about tinkering with life forms, especially **germline** cells, whose modifications are passed to offspring. Attention to the long-term implications of this work is called for.

Example sentences:

His group, which advocates for greater government regulation of synthetic biology, is often referred to as a bunch of luddites.

He is excited by the potential of a project in the synthetic biology lab.

She felt like she had really contributed to the field of synthetic biology after her first submission to the parts registry.

Quotes:

"The underlying goal of synthetic biology is to make biology easy to engineer. What does that mean? It means that when I want to go build some new biotechnology, whether it makes a food that I can eat or a bio-fuel that I can use in my vehicle, or I have some disease I want to try and cure, I don't want that project to be a research project. I want it to be an engineering project."
— Drew Endy, Associate Professor, Bioengineering, Stanford University

 "Synthetic biology frees the design of life from the shackles of evolution." — Craig Venter, President & Chairman, J. Craig Venter Institute

"Synthetic biology seems to involve a quest for a degree of control over the basic mechanisms of life that human beings have never attained before."
— Stuart Russell, Professor of Computer Science, University of California at Berkeley

"Synthetic biology, at this moment, I think, is at the same point in time as silicon was back in the 1980s." — Bill Liao, European Venture Partner, SOSV

"What we achieved in that project was to put together some DNA which allowed bioluminescence, to show that it worked in [the bacterium] E. coli, and to submit it to the 'parts registry' which holds this DNA so anyone else can use it in future." — Theo Sanderson, PhD Student, Wellcome Trust Sanger Institute

Brain-Computer Interface

A **brain-computer interface (BCI)**, sometimes called a **direct neural interface (DNI)**, **synthetic telepathy interface (STI)**, or **brain–machine interface (BMI)**, allows for direct communication between the brain and an external device. BCIs are directed at assisting, augmenting, or repairing human cognitive and/or sensory-motor functions. The interfaces of any processing system, including the brain, are sensors and actuators, so it should not be surprising that these applications primarily take input from or provide instruction to prostheses that provide hearing, sight, and movement once *trained* to respond to electrical impulses in the brain. Likewise, due to the brain's cortical plasticity, the BCI can handle signals from the implanted interfaces as if they were natural sensory organs. In addition to working with prostheses, BCIs can bypass damaged nerve tissue to reach functioning body parts (as for example, in treating Parkinson's disease).

One goal of research in this field is to reduce the invasiveness of these devices. Unfortunately, for some purposes it is still necessary to place electrodes beneath the subject's skull. Another challenge involves accessing the appropriate signal without interference. Progress is dependent upon continuing growth of knowledge of the brain and how it represents information, using techniques such as **functional magnetic resonance imaging (fMRI)** and **diffusion tensor imaging (DTI)**. By analogy to the Human Genome Project, the Human Connectome Project looks to build a neural map of the brain.

Beyond restoration of human limbs and sensory organs, the technology could potentially be used to interface with any mechanical device, such as a keyboard or computer screen, or perhaps an Internet-connected computer. More nefarious applications, however, could intercept and interpret these electrical impulses to read thoughts or even generate them to implant false memories. Fortunately, due to the complexity of the brain, such developments are not yet realistic—but one might be alarmed and/or thrilled at how far we have already come.

Example sentences:

My aunt was given a BMI device to help her walk in spite of her Parkinson's disease.

She thought it was really cool that by using a BCI she could play the video game with no hands.

Maintaining our privacy is hard enough in the absence of STIs.

Quotes:

"It may sound like geeky mumbo-jumbo today, but, considering the pace at which new tech is developed and deployed *at scale*, neural appliances and collateral damage resulting from the careless use of such, may become a real problem even earlier than it seems." — Alexander Kolesnikov, Kaspersky Labs

"Once the funding is secured and the requirements for the prize are finalized, the race will be on for companies and teams around the world to compete to make a major breakthrough in BCI." — Rod Furlan, Founder, Lucidscape Technologies

"Brain-computer interfaces are amazing; let's see how well they can be made to work. For the best ones, of course, you need an implant, but if non-contact brain-computer interfaces get better that would be marvelous." — Andrew Blake, Distinguished Scientist & Laboratory Director, Microsoft Research at Cambridge

"As BCI technology develops, we can expect it to increasingly serve the function of cognitive enhancement. I'm reasonably good at mental arithmetic and algebra, but I'd take an onboard calculator and computer algebra program any day. A neural interface to Google, Wikipedia and other online resources would be nice, too." — Ben Goertzel, Chief Science Officer, Aidyia Limited

Nanotechnology

The genesis of the field of **nanotechnology** is credited to Richard Feynman, who in 1959 postulated a series of machines constructing ever smaller machines. Nanotechnology is the manipulation of matter on a scale of at least one dimension from 1 to 100 nanometers (nm). A nanometer is one billionth of a meter, about the width of three or four atoms (the average human hair is about 25,000 nm. wide). It is now possible to image, measure, model, and manipulate matter at **nanoscale**. Nanotechnology leverages the unusual physical, chemical, and biological properties exhibited by substances at the nanoscale. **Microelectromechanical systems (MEMS)** are of dimensions a thousand times larger than **nanoelectromechanical systems (NEMS)**. **Soft nanotechnology** is a convergence of *synthetic biology* and nanotechnology, inspired by the amazing machines in our cells.

Obviously, nanotechnology enables the creation of objects that will operate in very small spaces; an example would be delivering drugs within small blood vessels. Perhaps less obviously, it becomes possible to change the properties of materials by changing their internal composition. Materials can be made stronger, lighter, better or worse conductors of heat or electricity, more or less smooth, and/or more or less reactive. Properties such as magnetism and light reflectance can be modified. The possibilities for remaking existing products and imagining new ones are numerous.

Eric Drexler prognosticated precise molecular manufacturing (aka **nano-facturing**) via self-replicating nanorobots constructed bottom-up, in contrast to Feynman's top-down approach—a vision now referred to as **molecular nanotechnology** (MNT). Drexler first stoked and later tried to extinguish fears of these devices turning the universe into **grey goo**. Other concerns about nanotechnology include the impact of **nanopollutants** on the environment and the invasion of privacy through virtually undetectable surveillance devices. Yet nanotechnology presents profound opportunities for *disruption*, as has been promised for decades. Its time may be arriving.

Example sentences:

This new nanotech sunscreen with zinc oxide really works well, and you can't even see it on my skin.

Nanotechnology will one day make golf balls fly straighter!

She is concerned about health issues from nanoparticles in cosmetics.

Quotes:

"When a nanotech company matures and becomes a real business, it becomes something else. It becomes a biotech company or a cleantech company or a memory chip company. Nanotechnology has fueled the core innovations in electronics and energy." — Steve Jurvetson, Managing Director, Draper Fisher Jurvetson

"The central problem I see with the nanobot self-assembler then is primarily chemistry. If the nanobot is restricted to be a water-based life-form, since this is the only way its molecular assembly tools will work, then there is a long list of vulnerabilities and limitations to what it can do. If it is a non-water-based life-form, then there is a vast area of chemistry that has eluded us for centuries." — Richard E. Smalley, Professor of Chemistry, Physics and Astronomy, Rice University

"We need to take seriously the prospects for molecular nanotechnology, personal nanofactories and nanorobotics, and attempt to understand the societal and political consequences of these technologies now, before it is too late." — Robert Freitas, Senior Research Fellow, Institute for Molecular Manufacturing

"Nanotechnology will let us build computers that are incredibly powerful. We'll have more power in the volume of a sugar cube than exists in the entire world today." — Ralph Merkle, Faculty, Singularity University

The Singularity

Computing pioneer John von Neumann remarked about "ever accelerating progress in technology and changes in the mode of human life, which gives the appearance of approaching some essential singularity ... beyond which human affairs, as we know them, could not continue." Ray Kurzweil more recently popularized the **Singularity**, as a "merger of human technology with human intelligence," viewed as an inevitable consequence of general *exponential* technological growth, along the lines of von Neumann's usage. Indeed, we have experienced *disruptive* technological progress at ever-shortening *intervals*. Still, it seems unlikely that any particular *exponential* increase in technology (including *Moore's Law*) can be sustained indefinitely.

But the eventual ability of our computer programs to improve themselves would itself lead to *exponential growth*. Such an **intelligence explosion**, as posited by Irving John Good, would enable our computer programs to rapidly accelerate in effectiveness beyond human capabilities and beyond any human ability to foresee or control. The word "Singularity" is an implicit reference to gravitational singularities (as in black holes) and their inherent inscrutability. Likewise, as expressed in Vernor Vinge's **event horizon**, we cannot envisage a world designed by those so much more intelligent than ourselves.

Parallels with end-of-times theology are considerable, including disagreements over both when the Singularity, **the rapture of the nerds**, can be expected and whether it will be a doomsday scenario or an exhilarating one. Some recommend mechanisms to avoid situations of "runaway" intelligence. Others foresee a merging of organic and inorganic intelligence (involving *BCI*) rather than a competitive strain of intelligence. Others emphasize the serious, immediate implications of accelerating technological progress: severe inequality between those who can apply it productively and those who cannot.

Example sentences:

He believes that the potential dangers of the Singularity are every bit as real as those of nanotechnology or synthetic biology.

Will the Singularity bring Nirvana or the ruin of civilization?

From her mainstream perspective, many Silicon Valley leaders' concern with the Singularity seems excessive.

Quotes:

"The Singularity denotes an event that will take place in the material world, the inevitable step in the evolutionary process that started with biological evolution and has extended through human-directed technological evolution." — Ray Kurzweil, Director of Engineering, Google

"That the singularity will happen is a fact ... It's like watching an avalanche rolling down a hill." — Vernor Vinge, Professor of Mathematics, San Diego State University (retired)

"Ray Kurzweil and others are predicting that there's a tidal wave coming. But they say it's bliss—it's not bad, it's good, at least if you're surfing it in the right way. If you own the right kind of surfboard, it'll be fun." — Douglas Hofstadter, Author, *Gödel, Escher, Bach: An Eternal Golden Braid*

"The singularity will either be really successful, in which [case] we're going to have the biggest boom ever, or it is probably going to blow up the whole world." — Peter Thiel, Managing Partner, Founders Fund

"I think that the 'Singularity' has become a suitcase word with too many mutually incompatible meanings and details packed into it, and I've stopped using it." — Eliezer Yudkowsky, Decision Theorist

MARKETING

Pain Point

Customer **pain points** are the specific problems that businesses seek to address with their products or services. Pain points are the most consistent and significant motivators behind customers' purchases. Products that address only things that would be "nice to haves" for the customer are unlikely to generate much sales volume. For that reason, Silicon Valley investors regard a compelling description of the customer's pain points, and how the company intends to address them, as essential components of a solid *pitch* and *business plan*.

Identifying customer pain points accurately involves finding the root cause of the problem faced by the customer through understanding what customer goals are frustrated by the problem and how it affects the person or company on a daily basis. Finding pain points can often be tricky, because in many cases customers do not articulate them clearly and may not even be fully aware of them, especially if they relate to missed opportunities.

Spending time with customers is a good way to discover pain points. It is key to ask open-ended questions and truly listen to the responses. Anthropological techniques, such as observing customers in their own environment using the currently available technology, are also effective in helping uncover customer pain points.

The way in which a *startup* intends to address customer pain points is known as its **value proposition**. Ideally, a value proposition will be specific enough to enable a customer to determine whether or not the *startup* has indeed delivered it, and will clearly distinguish the *startup* from its competition.

Successful *founders* have often been motivated by a desire to address a pain point with which they have had personal experience.

Example sentences:

We plan to get out of the office and visit customers more so that we can learn about their pain points.

As a salesperson, she is well positioned to understand the customers' pain points.

We need to know where the customer pain points are in order to make sure our product actually serves a real customer need.

Quotes:

"When you fully understand [buyers'] pain points and needs and can align them with a clear offer and comprehensive benefits, the sales nurturing process will leapfrog ahead." — Dan McDade, CEO, PointClear

"We basically went back to the drawing board and asked, 'How do we address these two pain points for small to medium businesses?' With this intent in mind we said, 'Okay, let's come out with a bundle that is a hardware-software solution that would alleviate some of these customer pain points.'" — Sam Mahalingam, CTO, Altair Engineering

"'Pain point' is the business term for emotion, and emotion is a term that leads to business conversions." — Laura Hancock, CFO, Content Equals Money

"Valuable as finding the pain point is, a surprising number of entrepreneurs mess up the process. In some cases, you think you already know the problem. In other cases, you're not paying attention to the right signs. This subtracts from your precious time and wastes a great customer interview." — AJ Agrawal, CEO, Alumnify

Positioning

Positioning aims to place a brand or product in a distinct market position, relative to its competitors, in the mind of the customer. This may involve creating a specific image, such as luxurious or practical, inexpensive or premium, traditional or trendy, sporty or fashionable, etc. It may also involve emphasizing features that distinguish it from competitors.

Positioning assumes segmentation and targeting. **Segmentation** is the partitioning of the full market into **market segments** consisting of potential customers with similar needs and behavior. **Targeting** is the selection of a particular segment, the **target market**, for the firm to address because of its profitability, accessibility, or because the firm has some competitive advantage there. The sequential application of segmentation, targeting, and positioning is denoted by the acronym **STP**.

Key elements of positioning include researching the needs and wants (both substantive and psychological) of the target market in exhaustive depth; defining the *pain points* specific to the target market that the product or brand aims to address; and identifying exactly how the product or brand addresses the situation in a better way than competitors.

To position itself consistently, a *startup* will create a **positioning statement,** which succinctly (in a single sentence) communicates what problem it intends to solve for whom and how it will do so. This positioning statement should clearly differentiate it from competitors in the same market (e.g., by lower-cost or superior product). Another aspect of positioning is whether a company plans to sell only the few items wanted by many or go for the **long tail**, i.e., the many items each of which is desired by only a few.

A startup's positioning is often initially conveyed through names—of both its products and the startup itself. Startup names tend to follow trends such as containing "Zen" or ending in "ly" or "ify," often as one batch of available Internet domain names after another is exhausted. Some names are directly expressive of positioning; others are meaningless, creating a blank slate upon which a brand can be defined (and making it easier to obtain an Internet domain). Positioning is also conveyed through various forms of marketing materials and advertising, as well as the product itself.

Example sentences:

We considered various market segments before settling on gambling addicts.

Having realized that their target market was in need of social connection, they emphasized those aspects of their product.

The product's poor quality defeated its positioning as a luxury item.

Quotes:

"You need to position your product in the mind of your user. And that requires taking your potential users into account, assessing the product's strengths and weaknesses, and considering your competition." — Arielle Jackson, Marketing and Communications Consultant

"Many startups do a poor job explaining crisply what they do, especially during their early stages. They often confuse or ignore messaging, positioning, and branding." — William Mougayar, Founder, Startup Management

"To scale efficiently and effectively, expansion-stage companies need to focus their efforts not on a broad universe of potential customers, but rather on a specific subset of customers who are most similar to their best current customers. The key to doing so is through customer segmentation." — Tien Anh Nguyen, Director of Market Insights, Openview Venture Partners

"You want to be a big fish in a small pond. If you are a small fish in the market you are addressing, you need to shrink the pond so you can appear bigger. You need to be very specific about the companies you are targeting..." — Aaron Ross, Author, *Predictable Revenue*

Total Addressable Market

Total addressable market (**TAM**) refers to the revenue opportunity available for a particular product or service. If the market is established, TAM can be calculated as the sum of revenues for all companies selling the product or service. Otherwise, the TAM must be estimated by considering the extent of the market that the company could hope to serve and how much customers in that market would be willing to pay.

Since TAM gives a company a quick metric of the potential revenue opportunity for a product or service, identifying it helps a company (and its potential investors) validate a particular business opportunity or prioritize between several of them.

While TAM is a useful indicator of long-term potential, a company must be realistic about what it can achieve at any point in time. **Serviceable Available Market (SAM)** is the portion of the TAM a company intends to *target* given the characteristics of that *market segment*, constraints and features of the current offering, the available distribution channels, and the market position of competitors. A distinction is sometimes made between SAM and **Serviceable Obtainable Market (SOM)**, where only SOM takes into consideration distribution channels and competition. These descriptors can serve as goals that a *startup* might try to achieve in claiming market share, with TAM as the longest-term goal and SOM as the shortest.

TAM and SAM are important metrics for investors, who need a sense of the size and rate of growth of the market for the company's product or service. A *startup* that has a solid understanding of the long and short-term potential of its market, and can provide reasonable figures for both TAM and SAM, is more likely to attract capital investment.

Example sentences:

They pitched sky-high TAM numbers, but were light on strategy.

The company's new product suite extended its SAM.

Although the company's TAM is tremendous, the small SAM made them doubt whether it has a clear path forward.

Quotes:

"Many first-time founders fail to understand the difference between the potential of the [TAM] and the very finite subsection they can hope to capture. No company ever captures the entire market they pioneer." — Jay Samit, Serial Entrepreneur and Author, *Disrupt You!*

"This acquisition expands our value proposition for sales forces into CPQ, which doubles our total addressable market for our overall product suite." — Leslie Stretch, President & CEO, CallidusCloud

"So entrepreneurs, here's my advice... don't just settle for an IDC or Gartner generated number ... Figure out your TAM, SAM and SOM for yourself. Show a calculation ... Prove to me that you have a more granular understanding than what IDC or Gartner has provided." — Steve Berg, Senior Analyst, RTP Ventures

"It's not the total size that gets me most excited, it's the Addressability. How are you going to acquire your customers and what insights or unfair advantages do you have in doing so?" — Hunter Walk, Partner, Homebrew VC

"They were asking questions about our diagnostic of the total available market. We were talking about building the most important company in the world." — Alex Karp, CEO, Palantir

Customer Acquisition Cost

Customer acquisition cost (**CAC**) is the total average cost of persuading a customer to buy a company's product or service. Expenses related to sales and marketing (including salaries, travel, public relations, *SEO*, and advertising) are matched to the time period over which they are effective and divided by the number of customers attained in that period. If a company cannot sustain the various costs while its potential customers enter and move through the acquisition cycle, its survival will be in question.

The CAC is offset by the **lifetime value** of a customer (or **LTV**), which is a prediction of the net profit expected from the entire future relationship with the customer—the immediate and any recurring revenues expected from the purchase and any future upgrades, less the predicted costs associated with providing those products.

The ratio of LTV to CAC is important, as is the time frame over which the LTV is recovered. High CACs or too long an LTV recovery period can inhibit *startups* from *scaling*. CACs can accumulate rapidly if increasing amounts of human capital must be deployed to close each deal. *Startups* often underestimate CAC, but investors are quite aware of this pitfall and tend to be skeptical of the optimism expressed by *entrepreneurs* in this area.

One way to lower CAC is to concentrate on optimizing every stage of **customer conversion**; *VC* Dave McClure identifies the **"Pirate" metrics** as **AARRR**: (user) Acquisition, Activation, *Retention*, Referral, and Revenue. For *SaaS* models, *freemium* can be effective in lowering CAC, since it encourages customers to come to the firm, but both the costs of providing the free service and those of converting the free customers to paying ones must be accounted for.

Example sentences:

The long sales cycle led to a high CAC.

Although they had high customer LTV, it did not pay off in time to cover their CAC.

Free trials have proven successful in reducing our CACs.

Quotes:

"About 10 percent of people who clicked the mobile ad signed up for the service. Our customer acquisition cost dropped from $30 to 10 cents over-night." — Omar Hamoui, Partner, Sequoia Capital

"There aren't that many customer lifetime values that are on par with a $6 acquisition cost. That's mythic. In fact, it's going to be very tight for most developers at $2." — Andrew Green, Head of Business Development and Business Operations, TinyCo

"It doesn't take a genius to understand that business model failure comes when CAC (the cost to acquire customers) exceeds LTV (the ability to mone-tize those customers." — David Skok, General Partner, Matrix Partners

"You can have a high customer acquisition cost and relatively high sales price but low sales cycle which trends toward a high average revenue per customer/user (ARPU)." — Chaney Ojinnaka, Founder & CEO, ChalkRow

"I can't believe how many startups I see driving up their cost of customer acquisition with just this one mistake: no clear list of target customers." — Danielle Morrill, Co-founder & CEO, Mattermark

Network Effect

A **network effect** exists when the *value* of a product or service is dependent upon the number of people using it. A product or service with a positive network effect will increase in *value* for all users with each additional user (or active user). As the number of users, and thus the *value* delivered, rises, more users flock to it.

The traditional example of network effect, generally known at the time and since formalized as **Metcalfe's Law**—is the telephone. The more households with telephones, the more *value* a telephone has to anybody who owns one. Users of social networks receive similarly increased benefit as other users join, since they have access to more people's posts, and more people have access to theirs. Systems with a network effect can leverage their users who would benefit from growth to *go viral*.

Network effects lead to an aura of inevitability once a certain number of users, referred to as a **critical mass**, is reached. According to Robert Metcalfe, critical mass is achieved when the *value* of the product or service exceeds the price paid.

Much of the Valley's emphasis on *Agile methodologies* is motivated by the race among competitors to be **first to market**. The resulting **first mover advantage** is in large part an opportunity to reach critical mass.

With a network effect, the more users a business has, the greater a *barrier to entry* is created, since any potential competitor will be handicapped until they reach a similar market share. A more global definition of critical mass might be the capture of a large enough portion of the market that potential competitors will be in the unfortunate situation of being able to catch up only by winning over customers from the leader, which is quite difficult since by assumption they offer less *value*. Competition, however, is often not quite so direct.

Example sentences:

He was looking to start a social business because they tend to benefit from network effects.

He is not bothered by the monopolies caused by network effects, because consumers reap much of the benefit.

Their dating site intended to capitalize on a network effect.

Quotes:

"Network effects can be powerful, but you'll never reap them unless your product is valuable to its very first users when the network is necessarily small ... Paradoxically, then, network effects businesses must start with especially small markets." — Peter Thiel, Managing Partner, Founders Fund

"Establishing a nucleus of critical mass in something then allowing network effects to play off of that can be very powerful. Leverage the community to amass local knowledge and provide services for one another." — Nate Blecharczyk, Co-founder & CTO, Airbnb

"Anti-network effects occur when a community [that] has already achieved critical mass begins to lose value with each additional signup. The reason is that the core community that created the value to begin with starts to get marginalized and leaves." — Dalton Caldwell, Partner, Y Combinator

"If there is one altar at which Silicon Valley worships, it is the shrine of the holy network effect. Its mystical powers pluck lone startups from obscurity and elevate them to fame and fortune." — Sangeet Paul Choudary, Founder & CEO, Platform Thinking Labs

Growth Hacking

Growth hacking is a mindset through which smaller tech companies do everything possible to stand out in a big market, gain exposure, and increase their user base. Growth hacking differs from standard marketing in that it bypasses the traditional corporate structure and techniques of a marketing team—in part because the *startup* cannot afford them and in part because it can achieve greater results in other ways. In 2010, Sean Ellis, Founder and CEO of Qualaroo, coined the term "growth hacker" in a blog post. Sean defines a growth hacker as "a person whose true north is growth. Everything they do is scrutinized by its potential impact on *scalable* growth."

Growth hacking looks intensely at the business and leverages every opportunity and resource toward growth. This can involve skillful use of *viral loops*, content marketing, *search engine optimization*, **social media marketing** (using social networking websites to gain brand awareness or website traffic), and email marketing. Growth hackers make extensive—and often creative— use of the many low-cost and free tools currently available for doing business online. Growth hacking is a modern version of **guerrilla marketing** that is implemented on the web by technologists rather than on the streets in front of a live audience. The word *hacking* gets across the blurring of the lines between marketing, product, and engineering, and a "do-whatever-it-takes" attitude toward making growth happen despite resource constraints.

Growth hacking also relies on strategic and evidence-based decision-making. Proper **A/B testing** can help a growth hacker make these decisions by comparing two versions of a concept to see which most effectively generates the intended result, whether that be sales, increased time on the site, return users, notifications to other users, referrals to potential users, or anything else related to growth.

Example sentences:

It is important for growth hackers to look beyond social media.

Growth hacking enabled us to attract a lot of customers without a huge marketing budget.

Through growth hacking, he felt that he had refined the firm's viral messaging to a science.

Quotes:

"Among the benefits of a successful growth hacking strategy is that you are able to reduce churn, which means that you can maximize the users you're acquiring and retain a higher percentage of them." — Brett Relander, Founder, Launch & Hustle

"Growth hackers champion experimentation. A/B testing, landing page optimization, paid media tweaks, email subject lines. These are good tactical things to do; and when done well, the tactics can help startups achieve relevance with potential customers." — Kavi Guppta, Founding Partner, WEDOTHAT

"In Silicon Valley, people talk a lot about growth hacking, which I think is obnoxious, but it's become a meme. Growth hacking is really a fancy term for engineered spam. It's a consumer anti-benefit, but it's necessary to building critical mass." — Bing Gordon, Partner, Kleiner Perkins Caufield & Byers

"Growth hacking appeared as the modern way in the age of Web 2.0 to reach a market and distribute an idea. Instead of classic marketing which typically interrupts your day, a growth hacker uses 'pull'; he or she understands user behavior provides value immediately to persuade. A growth hacker wraps messaging into the fabric of the lives and thoughts of users." — Aaron Ginn, Co-founder, LincolnLabs

Thought Leader

A **thought leader** is a person or organization widely recognized for expertise in a specific field. Being a thought leader, however, is *not* the same as knowing the most about a topic. Thought leaders stand out because their ideas are so innovative and they present them so well that they guide the thinking and decisions of others. Thought leaders are often among the primary "go-to" resources in their field. As a recognized authority, a thought leader is frequently sought out by peers, clients, and even competitors for knowledge, intuition, and advice.

Thought leaders gain and maintain their status by shaping the conversation around their areas of expertise, often by creating a steady flow of relevant and strategic **content** such as books, blogs, videos, and **white papers**. This process is called **content marketing** when it serves to promote offerings by the thought leader or their firm. Content marketing can help to establish thought leadership, boosting one's site's visitors and *SEO*, and ultimately increasing **lead generation** (stimulation of interest or inquiry from potential customers) and sales.

Careful curation of content is key to the effectiveness of content marketing and the likelihood of attaining thought leadership. **Curation** refers to the gathering, selection, and online presentation of content related to a particular theme, and may take place either on a company's site or through social media.

On a more individual level, thought leadership can be obtained via a commitment to **personal branding**, i.e., the application of marketing insights (in particular the care inherent in the notion of a building a brand) to one's persona and career. In this case, the personal brand would reflect expertise in the relevant subject matter.

Thought leadership can be so valuable to a company that it has even become a job category under the title **product evangelist**. This role involves seeking out speaking opportunities to inform the public of the benefits of the company's underlying technology.

Example sentences:

We attended a conference with thought leaders from Silicon Valley and now we're re-thinking our organizational structure.

As a thought leader in mining, he's often asked to speak at conferences.

That company was always successful, but became more so when their CEO positioned herself as a thought leader.

Quotes:

"Thought leadership is simply about becoming an authority on relevant topics by delivering the answers to the biggest questions on the minds of your target audience." — Michael Brenner, CEO, Marketing Insider Group

"Thought leadership is backed up by substance ... You don't just know how to get the car down the road, you know how the engine works." — Mary Meeker, Partner, Kleiner Perkins Caufield & Byers

"Unlike most forms of paid marketing, content marketing has a cumulative and compounding return." — Tomasz Tunguz, Partner, Redpoint Ventures

"View your personal brand as a trademark; an asset that you must protect while continuously molding and shaping it." — Glenn Llopis, Chairman, Glenn Llopis Group

Freemium

Freemium (a portmanteau that combines the words "free" and "premium") describes a *business model* in which a business gives away a core product to a large user base and then sells premium upgrades to a smaller fraction of this base. A freemium model is not simply a free product, but an array of products and services with different user levels.

Unlike a free trial, which allows a user to test a product or service for a limited time before buying, a freemium offering is comprised of a product or service that is *always* free and an array of additional products or services available for a fee. These premium products or services might include proprietary features, functionality, or virtual goods. They may exempt the user from advertising that is presented in the free version or provide control of the visibility of the user's information beyond what is provided there.

Due to the increasing accessibility and decreasing costs of digital production, freemium *business models* are quickly gaining ground in multiple industries, including publishing, music, and education. The freemium model is especially common in web-based services with *SaaS* delivery, smartphone apps, and mobile games. Somewhat of a digital version of a loss leader, freemium is facilitated by the fact that marginal costs for software are near-zero. In some cases, such as business social network LinkedIn, freemium goes beyond a loss leader in that the free users actually add value for the premium users, via a *network effect*.

Some businesses find it economical to transfer to a freemium model only after developing a base of paying users. In any case, a freemium model must walk a fine line—provide too much value in the free version and have difficulty converting users or not enough value and be accused of deception.

Example sentences:

Skype has one of the most well-known and longest-running freemium models.

The company had to back out of its freemium model after being unable to convert users.

The VC questioned whether the freemium model startup could extract more value from its non-paying customers.

Quotes:

"The decision to move away from freemium was the best business decision we ever made." — Lance Walley, Co-founder & CEO, Chargify

"Recall that one of the chief purposes of freemium is to attract new users. If you're not succeeding with that goal, it probably means that your free offerings are not compelling enough and you need to provide more or better features free." — Vineet Kumar, Assistant Professor of Marketing, Yale University

"Freemium is really a construct of the digital age because there's almost no marginal cost to digital goods." — Chris Anderson, Author, *Free: The Future of a Radical Price*

"If you are looking to build a lifestyle business that'll make you $8,000 a month and you have a good product, you can probably do without Freemium. If you want to build a dominant company that has a substantial market share, Freemium can help you accelerate adoption." — Uzi Shmilovici, Founder & CEO, Base CRM

Enterprise

Enterprise, as an adjective, refers to products, services, or marketing approaches aimed at corporate users (in contrast to **consumer**, which denotes products, services, or marketing approaches aimed at individuals). Two related terms are **business-to-business (B2B)** and **business-to-consumer (B2C)**, indicating that a company sells to other businesses or directly to consumers, respectively. **Multisided** business models address multiple forms of users simultaneously.

"Enterprise" may be added to various phrases to indicate a version aimed at companies, with the connotation of meeting the needs of the company as a whole. **Enterprise resource planning (ERP)** systems handle functions such as finance, operations, and logistics. **Enterprise social software** provides social media functions within a company. **Enterprise marketing management (EMM)** is a category of software that includes marketing dashboards, campaign management, lead management, and *predictive analytics*. **Enterprise portals**, also called **enterprise information portals (EIPs)** are web portals that integrate information, people, and processes across organizational boundaries. By analogy to the Internet (actually the World Wide Web built over it, but Enterprise Wide Web was deemed too clunky), an **intranet** supports communication and delivers *content* within a firm via tools often including a *wiki*. Steven Telleen coined the term while at Amdahl, intending that such systems appropriately control published material while ensuring that it is easily found and properly interpreted.

In the past, enterprise products were intended to be run on a company's own servers, making them very expensive. The emergence of *SaaS* has made it possible for **small and medium-sized businesses (SMB)** to take advantage of enterprise software.

With *IT consumerization*, enterprise products look increasingly like *consumer* ones, but both their underlying requirements and their marketing and *monetization* strategies are likely to differ.

Example sentences:

Enterprise technology is being increasingly driven by the same trends seen in consumer technology.

Their startup started out as B2C, but now they are shifting their focus to B2B because it's more profitable.

The VC was surprised to be pitched by a consumer-oriented startup because everybody knew he focused on enterprise.

Quotes:

"One key difference is that a CEO of a consumer company really needs to understand customer acquisition through marketing channels vs. the CEO of an enterprise company who really needs to understand how [to] acquire customers through an enterprise sales force." — Todd Chaffee, General Partner, Institutional Venture Partners

"Enterprise sales and implementation cycles can also dramatically change how a business is run. Enterprises often go through extensive evaluations before choosing a product solution, which sometimes can take more than a year." — Alex Oppenheimer, Associate, New Enterprise Associates

"Consumers will be okay if Twitter crashes 10 times a day like they used to. If you have a mission critical piece of enterprise software, that thing cannot go down." — Aaron Harris, Partner, Y Combinator

"Enterprises are capitalizing on the consumerization of IT and proliferation of mobile devices by developing applications aimed at improving employee productivity and customer satisfaction." — Louis Columbus, Director of Marketing, eCommerce and Analytics, Apttus

Vertical

In general Silicon Valley parlance, **vertical** is used to refer to an industry in which a company might participate. The word **space** is used for the same purpose. Presumably both sound more hip than "industry." The businesses within a vertical develop and market similar products and services catering to particular customer needs. Further categorizations within a vertical are called **subvertical levels**.

Vertical, short for **vertical market**, however, can also stress the linear structure of the underlying *ecosystem* of interdependent companies. The series of companies adding *value* through a vertical is known as a **supply chain**. A supply chain traditionally extends from raw materials to the *consumer*. In the realm of software, a vertical tends to be organized by layers of abstraction, with *value* feeding up from low-level infrastructure through to user-facing apps. When considering advertising, the apps, as *content* publishers, lie below ad networks, ad agencies, and ultimately the advertisers seeking to reach *consumers*. **Vertical integration** is consolidation that is brought about through *acquisition* of companies within one's supply chain. By contrast, in a **horizontal market**, vendors serve a broad variety of industries or types of clients. An **infrastructure play** is an attempt to reach a horizontal market across the lower, infrastructure, level of various verticals. Software may be directed towards serving the specific needs of a particular vertical market (such as inventory management for car dealerships), or intended to be used horizontally across a variety of industries (such as a word processor or spreadsheet program).

In order to be successful in a vertical, a company must clearly understand the needs of the companies at every level within it, and ultimately of the *consumers*, to ensure that its offerings cater to those needs. In identifying and servicing such a niche, it may be able to protect itself from competition that is not similarly focused. That niche, however, can be both a limitation and a vulnerability.

A good strategy is often to start with one vertical market and then expand to others, at some point generalizing the offering to a *platform* for a horizontal market with add-ons for each vertical.

Example sentences:

They are aiming to dominate the pet care vertical.

We're working on a new project in the delivery space.

He believes that a startup should aim at becoming a clear leader in a particular vertical market.

Quotes:

"We're a first mover in a large, business-to-business vertical space." — Eddie Lou, Co-founder & CEO, Shiftgig

"When it comes to competing in the tech space, focus is certainly key. And one approach is to target a vertical—and hopefully, it is a large one!" — Tom Taulli, Founder, BizDeductor

"Taking a horizontal product and putting a light coat of vertical paint on it is rarely effective because customers won't find it credible. The best products for a specific segment were designed from the ground up for those segments." — April Dunford, Founder, Rocket Launch Marketing

"When creating a new product, one of the most important strategic decisions a startup can make is selecting the right vertical market to point all development and marketing resources towards." — Martin Babinec, Founder & Director, TriNet Group

Ecosystem

Just as organisms in nature exist within a biological community and a physical environment, organizations exist within an **ecosystem**, an economic community of interacting organizations and individuals with mutually symbiotic relationships, including producers, suppliers, customers, competitors, and other stakeholders. These various entities co-evolve their roles and capabilities over time. An ecosystem is likely to have a central company or companies—referred to as **keystone organizations**—that lead in setting the direction. For example, an ecosystem of firms surrounds Twitter, and Apple built an ecosystem of firms around its iPhone and iPad.

The nurturing and development of the ecosystem surrounding one's firm has become a key element in strategic planning; many successful firms have made this a priority. A healthy ecosystem can provide a company with greater public awareness, enhanced offerings, new customers, and new distribution channels. An ecosystem can be nurtured by helping network participants connect to each other more easily, or by sharing information or technologies with third party organizations.

By leveraging its ecosystem, a company can achieve more, and at larger *scale*, than it could on its own. For example, elements of an ecosystem may develop product components or accessory products or services. Development of a *platform* is a primary way to encourage the growth of an ecosystem.

Silicon Valley as a whole is regarded as having an *entrepreneurship* ecosystem that encourages the establishment and thriving of *startups*, including research universities, investors, and various specialized attorneys and advisors.

Example sentences:

The company might have survived had it been better able to nurture an ecosystem.

They vigilantly protect their product's ecosystem.

Many other regions have tried to duplicate Silicon Valley's entrepreneurial ecosystem without success.

Quotes:

"Technology entrepreneurs are increasingly building businesses that are deliberately anchored in platforms, communities, and business ecosystems." — Steven Muegge, Assistant Professor, Carleton University

"Many technology companies ... have built empires through their ecosystems. Google Analytics, for example, has spawned a whole economy of vendors, consultants and apps devoted to building on (and optimizing) its analytics." — Brad Mehl, President, Boundless Markets

"In Silicon Valley, there is a 'build it here, or build it nowhere' mentality, as ground zero for all great things in the technology scene, and access to its world class ecosystem." — George Deeb, Managing Partner, Red Rocket Ventures

"Many entrepreneurs consider Silicon Valley as the Leading Centre of Entrepreneurship. Unfortunately, entrepreneurs from outside the Valley fail to understand how and why the ecosystem works. They often underestimate the difficulty of reaching the right people and raising enough money, especially second and third rounds." — Ana Mihail, Director of Programs, Blackbox Accelerator, LLC

Monetization

A business **monetizes** by finding ways to leverage its assets in order to generate a liquid revenue stream. It is possible for an asset to be monetized in more than one way.

How to monetize is a key question that faces many *startups*, especially apps and websites that have gained large numbers of non-paying customers (their key asset) by offering free services and now must figure out how to make a profit from them. Even if a *startup* has built something that people love, it will not survive without persuading people to pay for it. Of course there's always advertising; as the old adage goes, if you're not paying for a product, you are the product.

Potential **monetization** methods vary widely depending on the nature of the company's business and the assets it possesses. Beyond advertising, methods of monetizing software could include charging add-on or membership fees based on the available feature set, license fees based on the number of users, or transaction fees based on the level of use.

Monetization is becoming an increasingly high priority for *startups*. While it used to be acceptable to spend a long time growing an audience or user base and worry about how to make money later, investors are now urging *startups* to show positive cash flow and strong margins sooner. This is consistent with *Lean Startup* methodology, where an ability to charge for a service is a form of validation of the *value* being provided. There is also increasing focus not only on *user acquisition* metrics but also on **customer engagement** and **retention** (via recurring revenue), as these are viewed as signals of monetization potential.

Example sentences:

The investors wanted to know how the startup was going to monetize.

In-app advertising must be unobtrusive for the customer if a startup is going to rely on it as a monetizing tool.

They have lots of users but still haven't figured out how to monetize.

Quotes:

"Perhaps the most clear-cut issue facing startups today, it seems, is the revenue vs. user base question. Since the meteoric rise of sites such as Facebook and Twitter, the majority of new tech startups, especially in the mobile and social space, have focused on building a following first, and worrying about monetizing that following later." — Omar El Akkad, Western U.S. Correspondent, *The Globe and Mail*

"If we're going to monetize Twitter, we have to make money everywhere the tweets go. The tweets go all over the place so how are we going do that?" — Dick Costolo, former CEO, Twitter

"Mobile game monetization is perhaps the hardest task in business and technology today. The lucky few, it seems, rake in millions of downloads and—without exaggeration—billions of dollars. The masses struggle by with a trickle of downloads and a few pennies here and there." — John Koetsier, VP Research, *VentureBeat*

"Given the difficulty of monetization for consumer products, ultimately the best way to get to breakeven isn't to try to optimize the 1% subscription rate to 2%, but rather to pick a huge market, create a killer product, and try to acquire millions of users." — Andrew Chen, Entrepreneur

"The mobile ad companies are wooing developers with various monetization models that can easily be integrated into an app with their SDK." — Rich Foreman, CEO, Apptology

Use Case

A **use case** describes how a system can be used in a given situation (i.e., case). Fundamentally, use cases define the various requirements of a system, but the concept is powerful enough, and the need to connect requirements with the actual system strong enough, that use cases can also organize other aspects, including tests, documentation, and even implementation.

Use cases define the system operation in terms of "who" (actors), "what" (actions), "when" (triggering events and preconditions), and "why" (goals), but not "how" (that is the purpose of system implementation). Use cases extend user stories, a staple of *Agile development methodologies*.

A **user story** describes simply, from the user's perspective, what they do and why. The standard template is: "As a ____, I can ____, so that ____. For example, "As a teenage Facebook user, I can control privacy settings so that I won't be embarrassed by my mother reading my posts." User stories can be prioritized to ensure that the most essential needs are satisfied. **Usage scenarios** allow for modeling a chain of interactions between various actors and the system.

The three formats have much in common, so "use case" is sometimes used generically for any of them. All define a single execution path through the system. In carving out a thin slice of work intended to make sense to both the customer and developers, they can form the basis of trust in a relationship that is often fraught with misunderstanding. Developing use cases at various levels of abstraction facilitates the task breakdown that is so important to budgeting. Doing so can also enable reuse, suggesting the class structure of the object-oriented program that may result from implementation efforts.

Example sentences:

The change to this use case will set back the project schedule.

We're looking at applying the technology to new use cases.

After testing the product on several use cases, we were able to develop a robust version.

Quotes:

"Listening to them describe their projects, it became quite apparent to me that there is a great deal of confusion regarding the definition, context and use of use cases." — Edward V. Berard, CTO, The Object Agency

"There are a lot of interesting ideas included in the bitcoin protocol, but ... it is going to go through iterations or should go through iterations of innovation before the powerful use cases are found." — Robert Sams, Founder & CEO, Clearmatics

"To understand a use case, you tell stories. The stories cover how to successfully achieve the goal, and how to handle any problems that may occur on the way. Use cases provide a way to identify and capture all the different but related stories in a simple but comprehensive way." — Pearl Zhu, Author, *Digital Master*

"In the technology world, your use cases are only as effective as the value someone's deriving from them. What seems obvious to you may not be to your developers or customers." — Darren Levy, VP Product, Ecommerce & Online Acquisition, TruConnect

User Engagement

Any web site needs to build **user engagement**, i.e., attract people, hold their attention, and keep them coming back plus, ideally, motivate them to recommend others.

Eyeballs refers generally to the number of people who view a website and are particularly crucial for media outlets and other websites whose profits are largely determined by the number of **page views** received. **Bounce rate**, the percentage of visitors who leave without interacting, and **user retention** levels, which indicate whether the same users keep coming back, are also measures of user engagement.

Author Nir Eyal identified a four-part loop that maintains user engagement:

1. Provide an **external trigger** (e.g., element in a news feed) that relates to some internal triggering mechanism (e.g., curiosity).
2. Facilitate a simple user action (e.g., clicking) in anticipation of a reward.
3. Provide the user with a reward (e.g., gossip) ideally linked to the internal trigger.
4. Facilitate user investment (e.g., rating of *content*) that helps to tailor future triggers.

Clickbait is a pejorative term for eye-catching headlines, external triggers that irresistibly beckon people to click-through to a site. Clickbait often works by piquing curiosity with provocative and/or incomplete information. Although clickbait *content* may not be authentic enough to sustain users' interest, some such headlines do generate significant forwarding activity on social media.

Web personalization maximizes user engagement by applying *predictive analytics* and *recommendation engines* to tracked browsing history and social activity so as to serve *content* that the user is likely to find interesting.

Example sentences:

The startup stayed focused on maintaining user engagement, sure that everything else would follow.

Delivering so many eyeballs, they make a fortune on display ads.

I can't believe I got suckered in by that clickbait.

Quotes:

"The term 'user engagement' can refer to any action taken by a user on a website such as posting a comment or a search query, filling in a contact form, signing up for a newsletter, etc. It also includes the time each user spends on a given website. Better user engagement leads to better conversion ratio, lower abandonment rates and potentially an increase in sales." — John Siebert, President, Bam Products

"For a to-do app an engaged user should be logging in every day to add and complete items whereas for an invoicing app an engaged user might only log in once per month. There is no consistent quantifiable definition of engagement across different products." — Des Traynor, Co-founder, Intercom

"People began to understand online publishing could generate more revenue from online eyeballs than the cost of audience acquisition." — Tolman Geffs, Co-President, The Jordan Edmiston Group

"In fact—and here is a trade secret I'd decided a few years ago we'd be better off not revealing—clickbait stopped working around 2009." — Ben Smith, Editor-in-Chief, *Buzzfeed*

"Habit-forming mobile marketing campaigns start with an external trigger that alerts users, AKA a push notification." — Bruno Bin Rodrigues, Marketing Director, Notificare

Virality

Just as a virus can spread quickly through a population as each infected individual in turn infects others, a company can grow its user base by leveraging existing users to sign on new ones. The company can also grow its fan base, or at least its name recognition, by leveraging existing fans to spread the word. Such **virality** will generate *exponential growth* in the user (or fan) base, either through guiding them to post on social media, or encouraging them to reach out directly (e.g., via email). The phenomenon was featured in a well-known 1980's TV commercial: "I told two friends... and they told two friends, and so on..." The "two" here is the **branching factor**, i.e., the *exponential growth factor*, and corresponds to the number of users that any given user can directly affect (in an extreme case, their entire address book!). Equally important is the **frequency** (inverse of the *exponential interval*), which indicates how often such telling takes place.

Viral loops are product features through which one user easily shares *content* with others. By contrast, **viral oops** (credited to Nir Eyal) are unintentional actions by users, enabled by apps, that notify a large number of other users, such as in the aforementioned address book slam.

A given piece of content or messaging, or a company's product or service, can be said to have **gone viral** when it has entered the public consciousness through virality. An idea that has gone viral is called a **meme**.

Virality is the goal of many social media marketing campaigns and marketers claim to have various techniques for achieving it. Yet unlike virility, there appears to be no "secret formula" for virality.

Nor can one control what goes viral—many of the biggest corporate social media slipups have involved things going viral that the company wishes had not.

Example sentences:

The new speed-dating app took only three days to go viral.

If you make a video with yoga and cats, it's sure to go viral.

The startup couldn't handle its viral growth and almost folded as customers got annoyed at the web site failing to load.

Quotes:

"Virality is contagious; and startup founders, recognizing that contagion can be spread intentionally as well as spontaneously, are increasingly adept at nurturing managed viral growth." — Paul Grossinger, Angel Investor

"If somebody says we've gotta make a campaign go viral, it's going to be a miserable failure because you're setting it up from the wrong perspective. If you're gonna make something go viral, make content that people want to consume." — Josh Cherfoli, Senior Manager, Growth Initiatives, HDE Marketing, HomeDepot

"The viral loop of people inviting each other to most social networks revolves around a user posting a widget to their page and having friends see their page." — Jia Shen, CEO, Mekalabo

"A quick look around all the B2C startups shows that, although viral growth is often hoped for, in reality it is extremely rare." — David Skok, General Partner, Matrix Partners

"The connotation "going viral" typically means having a viral growth coefficient of greater than 1. For every user that comes on your platform, he or she refers 1 additional user. This ensures a service will 'hockey stick.'" — Steve Cheney, Co-founder, Estimote

Native Advertising

Native advertising, familiar as product placement in film, provides **native content,** also known as **sponsored content,** designed to blend into (appear to be native to) the **organic content** central to the purpose of the medium in which is appears. The goal is to build trust and engage with potential customers in a way not possible through traditional advertising. To be maximally effective, the native advertising's *content* should engage with a select *target* audience via an area of interest and then marry the brand messaging to that *content*.

In publishing, native advertising may take the form of an **advertorial** prepared by an advertiser and presenting their message with the *look and feel* of the publication's **editorial content**. Where the message is more subtle, native advertising can approach *content marketing*. In either case sponsored content should be demarcated clearly to avoid deceiving the reader into thinking that it is editorial content, using a label such as "advertisement" or "promoted by" or "presented by," and possibly also including the sponsor's logo.

Native content may also stand in for *user-generated content*. In social media, native advertising takes the form of promoted tweets (on Twitter) or sponsored posts (on Facebook). An advantage of native advertising on social media is the possibility of the native ad being shared and *going viral*.

Publishers need to use care in selling native advertising, not just because of the potential for *consumer* confusion but because their own brand could be damaged—potentially more so than in other forms of advertising—by *content* offensive to their audience. More broadly, publishers will benefit from a **content strategy** that defines what is or is not appropriate, including for sponsored content.

Example sentences:

As an active user of social media, she was particularly good at creating native advertising for those sites.

As a Millenial, he has a different view of native advertising than people in older generations.

The news outlet relied on native advertising for monetization.

Quotes:

"As publishers look to these new forms of monetizable ad units, those who haven't built out a strong content strategy for what type of native content will appear will start to accept anyone's content, breaking one of the main rules of native: it must add value for the user, it must add value to the marketer by building a deeper more meaningful relationship with the users." — Mark Howard, Chief Revenue Officer, Forbes Media

"The challenge with native is finding that sweet spot between fitting in and standing out." — Patrick Albano, VP & Head of Advertising Solutions, Yahoo

"Native advertising is a disruptive technique that is positioned to change the advertising business model. It is alternatively being hailed as a breath of fresh air and a controversial, exploitative new tactic. It has, in fact, been both." — Mark Sherbin, Consumer Operations, Content & User Education Specialist, Google

"[Google's text-based advertising worked] because when you searched for something, the few ads that showed up alongside the 'editorial' results were useful ... as a result, Google became the most dominant Internet company in the world." — Om Malik, Partner, True Ventures; Founder, *Gigaom*

Community Management

Online community management (or simply **community management**) is the practice of building, guiding, and growing the community on a self-built web site (e.g., a custom social media site or a computer game) or a social media group or page on a third-party site.

Effective community management can benefit a company in many ways: nurturing a stronger connection with customers, leveraging customers to support each other, and improving *user engagement* and, thus, *retention*. As with more general **social media management**, it can also provide access to people's impressions of a brand or product, increase site traffic and *SEO*, and increase product sales.

Community management involves attracting people to join the community, encouraging them to be actively involved, ensuring that the community is a comfortable place for users that provides real *value*, and leveraging user feedback and analytics to improve the *user experience* with the company or with the community itself. Care in selecting the initial community members and the standards for interaction in the community are essential to community management; future membership and interaction will largely be determined by these decisions. Posting positive examples of interaction on the site and effectively **moderating** community members' communication, e.g., removing non-conformant *content*, can help in maintaining the standards.

Online community management is a growing profession still in its infancy. The presence or absence of a good **community manager** largely determines which online communities flourish and which wither.

Example sentences:

Community management helps them probe customer sentiment.

Have you considered setting up and managing an online community to build your brand?

They hired a community manager when they realized that they needed someone to track their site's user activity.

Quotes:

"Community Managers should think of themselves as 'Community DJs'— you've got to play the "records" the brand wants you to play but you've still got to ensure that the community has a good time." — Sean M. Aaron, Community Manager, Carrot Creative

"Much of community managers' day-to-day work involves motivating people to take action: liking, sharing, commenting, etc." — Meghan Peters, Strategic Partnerships, Facebook

"Community Managers have gone from being a quirky role ("you mean you get paid to tweet!") to a highly in-demand role, a part of everything from Fortune 500 companies to startups to non-profits." — Megan Berry, Head of Product Development, RebelMouse

"A good community manager is someone who actively engages in various conversations across the web about his or her company's products or services in order to uphold their brand's rapport; indeed, they interact with users and consumers on various social media channels, but they also go beyond that and attempt to learn more about each consumer's needs and desires." — Ronald Barba, Managing Editor, Tech.Co

Search Engine Optimization

Every web site wants to attract as much traffic as possible. The **organic results** of a search engine, a form of *organic content*, are those that are not paid for and thus ideally respond most directly to the user's query. **Search engine optimization** (**SEO**) is the attempt to improve the page rank of a website in a search engine's organic results so that it is more easily discovered by people who search the web, thus bringing more people to the site.

There are various ways to try to improve the SEO of a site. One is to make sure that it is search engine-friendly from a technical perspective—that it is mobile responsive, has descriptive tags, and has no broken links. Another is to ensure that it has high-quality *content* that is updated frequently, is rich in **keywords**, and that attracts **inbound links** from other sites (a measure that search engines use to gauge the quality of a site).

SEO techniques can be classified into two basic types. One is **white hat** techniques that conform to search engine rules and guidelines. The other is **black hat** techniques that attempt to improve the site's ranking in search results in ways that go against them, such as **keyword stuffing** (loading a webpage with significantly more keywords than would be present if a natural writing style were used) and including keywords that are invisible to the user.

The algorithms used by the search engines to rank pages in search results have a big impact on SEO. Google names major updates to its algorithm after animals, such as Panda, Penguin, and Hummingbird, and they are the subject of much attention and speculation.

Example sentences:

My boss hired a consultant to help improve our SEO.

I made my site mobile-responsive in order to improve my SEO under Google's new algorithm.

When Google changed its search algorithm, my site stopped appearing on the first page of organic search results.

Quotes:

"The days of SEO being a game outsmarting algorithms are over. Today content strategy and valuable, sustainable strategies are essential, not just tricks and links." — Adam Audette, Chief Knowledge Officer, RKG

"By exposing your content in social media to content creators you increase your chances of getting a backlink which then helps your SEO." — Neal Schaffer, Author, *Maximize Your Social*

"Good SEO work only gets better over time. It's only search engine tricks that need to keep changing when the ranking algorithms change." — Jill Whalen, Transformational Consultant, Jill Whalen Consulting

"All proper SEO research starts with target keywords. Based on your demo-graphic and an in-depth analysis of current and recent search trends you can easily determine the keywords that have the most return with the least competition." — John Rampton, Founder & CEO, Due

"There's no set percentage for keyword density ... what you'll find is that if you continue to repeat stuff over and over again, then you're getting in danger of keyword stuffing, or gibberish and those kinds of things." — Matt Cutts, Distinguished Engineer, Google

HR AND WORK CULTURE

Acqui-hire

Startups often strive to be acquired by a large company. An **acqui-hire** (a portmanteau of the words *"acquisition"* and "hire") may not be what they have in mind. This form of *acquisition* is motivated by the procurement of the company's personnel (including, and perhaps only, the *founding team*), rather than its products or services, which may be discontinued following the acqui-hire. Typically, an acqui-hire involves a large company buying a much smaller firm.

In many cases, those who work for scrappy *startups* would never of their own volition have applied to work at a larger firm. So an acqui-hire may be the only way for a large company to access this desirable talent pool. An acqui-hire also enables a company to hire an intact team that it already knows works well together.

From a company's point of view, if its prospects are not good, an acqui-hire may be a face-saving alternative to shutting down, with the benefits of paying back investors and giving the *co-founders* and employees new and often lucrative jobs.

Acqui-hiring has achieved tremendous popularity throughout Silicon Valley, but it has also drawn criticism from those who believe that acqui-hires are not worth the costs (typically $1 to $1.5 million per employee), as employees hired in this way may not stay with the acquiring company beyond the length of their incentive package. Nevertheless, acqui-hiring has not abated; its supporters see it as a viable way to recruit talent in an increasingly competitive marketplace.

Example sentences:

Yahoo's heavy use of acqui-hiring has come under fire from detractors in Silicon Valley who are concerned that investors are not getting their money's worth.

An aggressive acqui-hire strategy makes sense in such a cut-throat recruiting marketplace.

As an acqui-hire, she got a much better deal than her friends who had applied for jobs directly.

Quotes:

"An acqui-hire is a way for companies to obtain good talent and—at least within the tech industry—is primarily focused on software engineers." — Gayle Laakmann McDowell, Author, *Cracking the Coding Interview*

"Google has been amazing at acqui-hiring, buying small companies for the engineers. I think in the competitive market of Silicon Valley, it's really a good way to do it. Big acquisitions often don't work out." — Ross Levinsohn, Board Member and Investor

"We feel like acqui-hire, right now it's really trendy, but we feel like that's failure." — Tipatat Chennavasin, Founder, Big Head Mode

"Acqui-hires probably aren't a very cost-effective way for the acquirer to recruit people, if you actually ran the math." — Jeff Fagnan, General Partner, Accomplice VC

"These days, many entrepreneurs consider an acqui-hire ... a safe alternative to company success." — Courtland Alves, Student Outcomes, Bloc, Inc.

Coworking Space

Coworking spaces, also known as **collaborative spaces** or **shared workspaces,** come in several varieties, with no clear boundaries between them. Some cater to individual members, others to *startup* teams, and many serve both. The former include *maker spaces*, which provide technical equipment and may sponsor projects or allow them to self-organize. The latter blend with those *incubators* and *accelerators* that provide office space along with any other funding or services. Coworking spaces may or may not offer dedicated work areas, but most provide shared meeting rooms that can be reserved. Some are primarily real estate providers that offer an official address and shared reception services. Some host lectures and other community events of interest to members. A **hackerspace** is a form of *collaborative* space where people gather to work on technical projects. They embody the hacker drive, but may engage in more patient explorations than the term hacker implies.

What they all have in common is that they are not just places to get your work done, but also places to gather and interact with like-minded people. Coworking spaces encourage creation of connections and collaborations among the people who use them. They are a great antidote to the loneliness, often faced by early stage *entrepreneurs*, of working at home or sitting by oneself in a coffee shop. Coworking spaces also provide an affordable alternative to regular office space for *startups* that comes with networking built in.

An Internet-based version of the shared workspace concept is the **online collaborative space**—an interconnected work environment in which the participants can have access to, and interact virtually with, other participants even if they are physically in completely different locations all over the world. Such teamwork is usually supported with electronic communications and groupware that help to diminish the usual obstacles of space and time differentials.

Example sentences:

He enjoyed being able to run difficult decisions by other members of his collaborative space.

Some freelancers are forming a co-working community.

Great projects keep coming out of that hackerspace.

She found that she was more productive when co-working.

Quotes:

"If we work at a traditional 9 to 5 company job, we get community and structure, but lose freedom and the ability to control our own lives. If we work for ourselves at home, we gain independence but suffer loneliness and bad habits from not being surrounded by a work community. Co-working is a solution to this problem." — Brad Neuberg, Product and Engineering Consultant, Dropbox

"Coworking spaces are created for the community and with the community in mind. It is not just a real estate business in which a physical space is rented: the role of the facilitator ... is to enhance the connections and interactions of the coworkers to bring them value and to actively accelerate serendipity." — Ramon Suarez, Author, *The Coworking Handbook*

"Today, careers consist of piecing together various types of work, juggling clients, learning to be marketing and accounting experts, and creating offices in bedrooms/coffee shops/coworking spaces." — Sara Horowitz, Executive Director, Freelancers Union

"Hackerspaces are the digital-age equivalent of English Enlightenment coffee houses. They are places open to all, indifferent to social status, and where ideas and knowledge hold primary value." — Heather Brooke, Author, *The Revolution Will be Digitized*

Brogrammer

Bro, short for "brother", is a slang greeting used predominantly among men to indicate camaraderie, and has also become a noun describing the men who use it. To some, the term suggests vapid men with a sense of entitlement and sexist attitudes. When combined with programmer to create the portmanteau **brogrammer**, it contrasts with the typical image of a programmer as being a *nerd* or a *geek*, and instead suggests a more macho, sociable, clubby image. Overall, the term brogrammer has come to represent how the preponderance of men in tech firms affects **corporate cultures**.

Diversity has emerged as a key concern in Silicon Valley, as statistics show that the majority of technical jobs at major firms are held by Caucasian or Asian males. The partnership ranks at *venture capital firms* and the executive teams of *startups* receiving funding similarly lack diversity. Some women, blacks, and Latinos feel that tech firms have cultures that marginalize them—due in part to male chauvinism and the influence of brogrammers.

For their part, tech firms explain that the lack of diversity in their ranks is largely a pipeline problem—there are not enough women, blacks, and Latinos who possess the necessary skills needed for their technical positions, so the culture is created by those with the greatest representation. Recent years, however, have seen an explosion of programs designed to expose girls and underprivileged minorities to **STEM** (science, technology, engineering, and mathematics) fields. Many firms also offer seminars to their employees designed to boost awareness of **unconscious biases**. It remains to be seen what impact such efforts will have on diversity and corporate culture in Silicon Valley's tech firms.

Example sentences:

She really hates the brogrammer culture at her workplace.

Recently, Silicon Valley firms have been getting blasted for their lack of diversity.

Silicon Valley is supposedly a meritocracy, but she thinks it's easier for brogrammers to get ahead.

Quotes:

"There's a rising group of developers who are much more sociable and like to go out and have fun, and I think brogramming speaks to that audience." — Gagan Biyani, CEO, Sprig

"For geeky men who never fit in socially, brogrammer culture may be reassuring in a way that more anodyne corporate cultures are not. Not only are the nerds finally on top, but they're encouraged to revel in their newfound status." — Kimberly Weisul, Editor-at-Large, *Inc*

"Based on the slightest interaction, we make a snap, unconscious judgment heavily influenced by our existing biases and beliefs. Without realizing it, we then shift from assessing a candidate to hunting for evidence that confirms our initial impression." — Laszlo Bock, SVP People Operations, Google

"There's a lot of people who are working on issues of diversity and inclusion in tech. Sometimes it can be difficult to work through, being one of a minority in the field, but just remember that software is an incredibly-powerful tool and it's worth sticking with, because you can do so much with it." — Tracy Chou, Software Engineer, Pinterest

H-1B Visa

The **H-1B** is a non-immigrant visa that allows U.S. employers to offer temporary employment (lasting three to six years) to foreign workers in "specialty occupations" which require highly specialized knowledge in a particular field and a bachelor's degree or its equivalent.

H-1B visas have provoked controversy for years. High-tech company executives justify expanding the H-1B visa program on the basis that it addresses the problem of a tech-worker shortage for which a failure of *STEM* education is the root cause. Critics, however, claim to the contrary that H-1B visas take tech jobs away from U.S. workers and give them to foreign-born ones, often in situations where they are held captive at far lower wage levels.

Rather few H-1B visas are officially available (although many organizations are exempt from the caps), and a large percentage of them are grabbed by Indian consulting companies who, it is claimed, use them to train their employees in U.S. jobs, replacing U.S. employees and lowering working standards, ultimately to return to India to compete against U.S.-based firms.

Larger Silicon Valley companies and their *VCs* have largely favored the H-1B visa program and frequently seek increases to the annual limit on H-1B visas in order to increase the labor pool of talented individuals. *VCs*, however, have another motivation to support immigration, as might we all. What does it take to leave one's country behind in the hope of achieving something better than that which others will settle for? Much of what it takes to be an *entrepreneur*. Indeed, 44% of Silicon Valley tech and engineering *startups* and over half of the *unicorns* were started by immigrants. The Blueseed project, which is currently on hold, sought to address visa restrictions by bringing foreign *entrepreneurs* to live on a ship moored off the coast of Silicon Valley just outside U.S. territorial waters, but within the range of local *VCs*. The issue of H-1B visas, and immigration more generally, is likely to remain controversial.

Example sentences:

If he loses his job he will need to go back home unless he can find another company to sponsor his H-1B visa.

He is angry that his Silicon Valley employer is lobbying for increases in the H-1B visa quota.

She considered suing her employer after she was replaced by a foreigner on an H-1B visa.

Quotes:

"I know from my experience as a tech CEO that H-1Bs are cheaper than domestic hires. Technically, these workers are supposed to be paid a 'prevailing wage,' but this mechanism is riddled with loopholes." — Vivek Wadhwa, Columnist, *The Washington Post*

"Hiring younger H-1Bs instead of older Americans means you save money." — Norm Matloff, Professor of Computer Science, University of California at Davis

"An outsourcing company can use American workers to train H-1B guest-workers, fire the American workers and outsource the H-1B workers to a foreign country where they will do the same job for a much lower wage." — Dick Durbin, U.S. Senator

"The H1-B program depresses wages for certain U.S. workers. It's rife with fraud and abuse. H1-B workers are vulnerable to discrimination, isolation, and exploitation. But the program is a necessary evil because skilled and enterprising new immigrants are exactly what the Bay Area economy needs." — Matthew Smith, Managing Editor, *City Pages*

"H-1Bs will remain in high demand as companies scramble to find workers to fill 560,000 empty tech jobs. For many computing and engineering vacancies, American workers are unavailable." — Adams Nager, Economic Policy Analyst, Information Technology and Innovation Foundation

BYOD (Bring Your Own Device)

BYOD, short for **Bring Your Own Device**, plays on the acronym BYOB, for Bring Your Own Bottle (i.e., bringing your own wine to a restaurant or party). It refers to a company policy that allows or encourages employee use of personal devices, such as smartphones, tablets, and laptop computers in the workplace to access sensitive company information. It is often regarded as an example and enabler of **IT consumerization**, the deliberate or accidental delegation of *enterprise* technology decision-making down to the individual employee users. Most employees have access to good technology at home and they increasingly expect the same at the workplace.

Many companies have accepted the inevitability of BYOD; a younger, more mobile workforce that grew up on the Internet is less likely to draw a line between professional and personal life, and indeed, Silicon Valley culture encourages such blending.

The BYOD trend has impacted the traditional IT Department, which in the past focused on providing employees with necessary technology. Under BYOD, IT must now decide how to protect its networks and how to manage technology not provisioned by the department. Due to the difficulties in doing so, it's been suggested that BYOD be replaced by more restrictive **CYOD (Choose Your Own Device)**, policies in which employees select from a limited number of "safe" options.

The term BYOD came into common use in 2009, when Intel recognized the growing tendency of their employees to bring their own devices into the workplace and use them to access the corporate network. Rather than reject this, as many other organizations had, Intel embraced it as a way to cut costs and improve productivity.

Example sentences:

We have a "zero tolerance to BYOD" policy at the workplace to protect company information.

Our company has begun to realize that it's nearly impossible to stem the tide of BYOD.

Although we have a flexible BYOD policy, office hours should be spent working, not surfing the web.

Quotes:

"Since BYOD programs often attract tech-savvy early adopters, help facilitate these pioneers by providing self-support tools." — Patrick Gray, Director of Digital Transformation, Cognizant Business Consulting

"Companies need to implement well-thought-out mobile device security and BYOD policies that do not get in the way of the pace of work but also do not compromise information security." — PJ Gupta, CEO, Amtel

"Like BYOD (Bring Your Own Device), traditional enterprises will need to adapt to developing policies and systems that integrate with—and potentially manage—many more devices than IT has ever worked with before." — Jason Hart, CEO, Identive

"We believe it's possible to maintain security while embracing BYOD." — Michael Lin, VP, Mobile Solutions, Symantec

"Some IT organizations today still cringe when employees, or even their own business users, come to them with the technology they want to use. To them BYOD (Bring Your Own Device) is just another four-letter word." — John Weathington, President & CEO, Excellent Management Systems

Perk

In Silicon Valley, companies wanting to hire talented and well-educated engineers, computer programmers, and other high-tech professionals must engage in the *war for talent*, competing in a highly competitive labor market. **Perks** (short for **perquisites**) give companies a tangible advantage in attracting—and, more importantly, retaining and motivating—the best and brightest that the region has to offer.

In general parlance, perks are nonstandard employee benefits such as free or subsidized housing, motor vehicles, daycare, and tuition reimbursement. The perks offered at some Silicon Valley companies, however, make these typical benefits seem meager. A kind of "perks arms race" has emerged in which companies attempt to outdo each other, providing increasingly lavish, complicated, and, perhaps, over-the-top favors for their employees. These include on-site gourmet meals, on-site arcades and candy shops, massage, yoga, and exercise classes, concierge service for dinner plans and home improvement projects, marriage counseling, and even egg freezing for female employees.

The ever-expanding list of potential perks available to employees has become so extensive that it has engendered a new staff position that manages the planning, sourcing, and provision of on-the-job perks: the **workplace services coordinator** or simply **workplace coordinator**.

Despite the Valley-wide preoccupation with perks, some criticize perk culture, arguing that these extra benefits make it difficult for an employee to voice concern or protest about other elements of their working conditions. They can also chain workers to the premises. Others have argued that perks make employees spoiled and entitled.

Example sentences:

Some believe that Silicon Valley perks have become too frivolous in recent years and are exacerbating wealth inequality.

The workplace services coordinator refused to go for his suggestion of a company-wide trampoline tournament.

The on-site bar perk sealed the deal for the recent grad.

Quotes:

"The goal with anything perks-wise is about making life easier. Work is stressful, you literally spend the majority of your life at work, so we want to create things that make their lives easier." — David Ulevitch, VP, Security Business Group, Cisco

"People in the rest of the country look at the Silicon Valley perks and think, 'What wonderful companies to work for' ... It's an arms race to come up with the jazziest rewards." — Gerald Ledford, Senior Research Scientist, The Center for Effective Organizations, University of Southern California Marshall School of Business

"The dirty secret of all these perks is it doesn't actually retain people or even attract people." — Laszlo Bock, SVP, People Operations, Google

"I have never really lusted after material things, and while rumors of free on-demand massages at the Google offices always made me smile, the allure of corporate perks was never enough to lure me." — Kate Harrison, Director of Merchandising & Eco-Friendly Marketing, mywedding

"Taking perks away is worse than not having them in the first place— especially if your culture is built on those things." — Dan Ruch, Founder, Rocketrip

Telecommuting

Silicon Valley firms have been leading the way in the recent trend of allowing employees to work from home, also known as **telecommuting**. Not only does this allow companies to portray themselves as offering better **work-life balance**, it may have other positive outcomes such as increased productivity and work satisfaction and decreased turnover. There are also environmental and health benefits from reduced commuting.

The increasing movement of work to *the cloud* and the convenience of **teleconferencing** systems and smartphone-based tools make it possible to work from anywhere. **Telepresence robots** can enable members of the **distributed workforce** to navigate group activities or anybody to attend a conference from afar. **Remote workers** can log in from the nearest coffee shop or *coworking space.*

Yet recently there has been a backlash against telecommuting among many Silicon Valley firms. It started with the much-decried 2013 announcement by Yahoo that it would abolish **work-from-home arrangements** as part of its efforts to re-energize its *corporate culture*. In justification, the internal announcement memo stated "Some of the best decisions and insights come from hallway and cafeteria discussions, meeting new people, and impromptu team meetings."

More recently and more quietly, others such as Google, Facebook and Apple have discouraged working from home. These and other large tech firms have invested significantly in building appealing headquarters offices that are designed to promote collaboration. There's a growing recognition that face-to-face interaction is the most effective way to foster teamwork and innovation. And indeed, recent research shows that working from home is only beneficial to employees and employers when it's done in small doses rather than all the time. So don't expect Route 101 to stop being a parking lot anytime soon.

Example sentences:

I'm going to be telecommuting tomorrow, so call me on my cell phone.

When I went back to work after my baby was born, I looked for a company that would negotiate a work-from-home arrangement.

It was unnerving having the telepresence robot sit next to me in the meeting.

Quotes:

"About three months ago, my company made the switch from a cozy office in the heart of Silicon Valley to going completely distributed. Now I usually work from home, as do my colleagues." — Robby McCullough, Co-founder, Beaver Builder

"During this critical turnaround period, HP needs all hands on deck. We recognize that in the past, we may have asked certain employees to work from home for various reasons. We now need to build a stronger culture of engagement and collaboration and the more employees we get into the office the better company we will be." — Meg Whitman, CEO, Hewlett Packard Enterprise

"A telepresence robot is like a two-way video-audio system on wheels. So you can see people; they can see you. You can talk to people, they can talk to you..." — Trevor Blackwell, Researcher, OpenAI

"More companies than not in Silicon Valley have poor work-life-balance because: (i) it's so competitive and expensive to live in Silicon Valley; and (ii) succeeding (in work, in business, in career, financially) and working hard are such [dominant values] in the culture." — Glenn Ballard, Lead Servant, Marpé Finance & Accounting

LIFESTYLE

Back-channeling

Silicon Valley is a dense network in which the players tend to know each other and to work through established networks. It is also a place that has embraced the benefits of data analytics, and thus, whether willingly or not, grown accustomed to transparency. The combination of these forces leads to the phenomenon of **back-channeling**.

The formally acknowledged means of any communication is the **front channel**. If one is applying for a job or for *VC* funding, there are standard materials, including a resume or *pitch deck*, respectively, that must be provided. A set of references is also generally on either list. Back-channeling involves going around those standard materials to get an "inside scoop." This may involve accessing references other than those provided, perhaps via information available on social media. It may also involve going to other, perhaps competing, firms to access their information through reciprocal, informal arrangements. The willingness of Silicon Valley companies to make back-channel agreements was recently on display in a settled class action antitrust lawsuit concerning collusive *anti-poaching* practices.

VC Mark Suster suggests that this game can be played both ways. Indeed, *VCs* look to back channels, such as networks of *founders* of their historic *portfolio companies*, some serving as *scouts*. *Entrepreneurs* can mobilize that network, not just to learn about *VCs* but to feed them information, including information regarding progress with other *VC firms*.

To some extent, back-channeling is a product of people's natural tendency to gossip; to some extent it reflects our current inability to address issues of privacy and data ownership.

Example sentences:

It was amazing what the VC found out about the founder through back channels.

The VC found some of the best companies in their portfolio through their back channel network.

The job candidate's social media postings provided ample fodder for back-channeling by potential employers.

Quotes:

"Hiring people who are way smarter than you and who have a lot more experience is actually really hard. ... you have to perform intense back channeling to truly understand how they operate and what kind of people they are." — Mikkel Svane, CEO, Zendesk

"That Silicon Valley's back-channeling is *invasive* hardly needs explanation. There's a general protocol around what is and is not appropriate for a prospective employer to research. ... There's a lot of information that is arguably potentially relevant to someone's future job performance that we, as a society, have rightly decided to be off-limits in making decisions about whether to hire someone." — Michael O. Church, Blogger

"And it was also very obvious that the VC community shared a lot of information. I think there was a lot of history with deals that had gone bad whether it was folks on the board or team members that we'd had. And so we spent probably, I don't know, four months and got very close to closing a number. We got really close with [a] number of VCs to close a round and they fell through last minute for different reasons. ... A lot of back channelling." — Richard Sim, Director, Monetization, Facebook

Maker Movement

The **maker movement** is a cultural phenomenon in which individuals apply **do-it-yourself** (DIY) principles to technology and engineering pursuits. The maker movement is characterized by informal, collaborative, and peer-led learning, with the primary goals being self-fulfillment and enjoyment—although the *monetization* of DIY projects and interests has a strong presence.

Some view the maker movement as a concerted reaction against the mass production and mass consumerism that have alienated individuals from the everyday objects they use. Others view it as an opportunity to leverage technology to benefit markets underserved by multinational corporations. Some just want to make cool things, have fun, and impress their friends.

A new technology that has galvanized the maker movement is **3D printing**, which represents some of the most salient features of the movement: low costs, widespread adaptability, and high innovation capacity. The ability of individuals to *prototype* their own hardware products by creating component designs and uploading them to a **3D printer** suggests a future in which customers create their own products at home instead of purchasing them in stores.

Maker spaces, also referred to as **fab labs**, are a form of *coworking space* where members of the maker movement (called **makers**) meet and **co-create**. Such facilities include small-scale workshops that feature digital fabrication equipment or other tools that help people transform ideas into reality. At the **Maker Faire**, a large convention, makers share and sell their products.

Co-creation occurring at *scale* is referred to as **collaborative production**, by analogy to *collaborative consumption*, and also has the potential to support new *business models*.

Example sentences:

The democratic and individualistic elements of the maker movement appeal to different parts of his personality.

He is going to be using his exhibit at the Maker Faire for his camp at Burning Man this year.

The technique for building miniature cars using 3D printing—that he perfected in the maker space—has become the basis of his new startup.

Quotes:

"What we see in the Maker movement is that a relatively small amount of people can have a big impact. You don't necessarily need the world's largest company behind you." — Dale Dougherty, Founder & Executive Chairman, Maker Media

"Making is fundamental to what it means to be human. We must make, create, and express ourselves to feel whole. There is something unique about making physical things. These things are like little pieces of us and seem to embody portions of our souls." — Mark Hatch, CEO, TechShop

"I think of the maker movement as being the web generation meets the real world." — Chris Anderson, CEO, 3D Robotics

"A Fab Lab today fills a room, weighs about 2 tons, and costs about $100,000. That includes 3-D scanning and printing, large-format and precision machining, computer-controlled lasers and knives, surface-mount electronics production, embedded programming, and computing tools for design and collaboration." — Neil Gershenfeld, Professor, Massachusetts Institute of Technology

Nootropic

Silicon Valley is all about pushing boundaries, including the physical limitations of the body. If we didn't get tired, lose focus, or need to sleep or eat, then we would have more time available to write code. Several trends in Silicon Valley aim at enhancing mental and/or physical capabilities, by applying the *DIY* experimental ethos of *hacking* to what we consume.

Nootropics, also known as **smart drugs**, build on the age-old college practice of cramming coffee along with calculus. In fact, Bulletproof Coffee, an invention of David Asprey inspired by the yak butter tea popular in Nepal, has become a staple of many *entrepreneurs* who swear that it boosts cognition. Nootropics are defined by their effects of enhancing cognitive function (reducing anxiety or improving memory, learning, or reaction time) while providing protection for the neural system. The latter attribute and lack of other side-effects distinguish them from amphetamine-based ADHD medication such as Adderall, also taken to boost productivity. The line between the neuroprotective and the neurotoxic is, unfortunately, quite hard to identify. The brand name of one nootropic sums up what many people seek from these substances: Unfair Advantage. Nootropics are often taken in combinations called **stacks**. In a related trend, taking **microdoses** (about one tenth of a "normal" dose, every fourth day) of psychedelics (such as LSD or mushrooms) is also reportedly catching on among techies who want to increase their energy and creativity.

The **paleolithic diet** is another way that many in Silicon Valley try to optimize their bodies. Based on the perhaps dubious idea that people should eat more like our caveman ancestors, the paleolithic diet eschews grains, beans, dairy, and refined sugars in favor of plenty of meat, fruits, and vegetables. Alternatively, those too busy working to prepare and eat normal foods may drink Soylent, a complete meal replacement designed to provide "freedom" from food.

Example sentences:

All their co-founders seem to believe that nootropics are the way to increase their edge.

Along with my nootropics regimen, I might start drinking Bulletproof Coffee to give me a boost of brain power in the morning.

He lived on nothing but Soylent for a week while on deadline.

Quotes:

"At this time of day, I'm typically struggling to stave off the post-lunch slow-down by downing another cup of coffee or two. But today, message after message is flying off my fingertips effortlessly—work e-mail, personal e-mail, digital errands I'd been meaning to run for months. I'm in the zone, as they say, and for this burst of late afternoon productivity, I might have nootropics to thank." — Kevin Roose, News Director, *Fusion*

"[A microdose is enough] to feel a little bit of energy lift, a little bit of insight, but not so much that you are tripping." — Rick Doblin, Founder & Executive Director, Multidisciplinary Association for Psychedelic Studies

"The Paleo diet is huge among tech people. Early adopting is one part of it, but there's probably an epidemic of bad eating among tech people who are working long hours, have sedentary jobs and are eating mainly pizza and fast food." — Dan Benjamin, Founder, 5by5

"We thought about doing Soylent drone delivery. Where you just hit a button on your phone and a drone comes and drops a bottle of Soylent, and you refuel." — Robert Rhinehart, CEO, Soylent

Quantified Self

Silicon Valley people love to gather and analyze data, and the **Quantified Self** (**QS**) movement, which started here, is focused on gathering and analyzing data relating to one's bodily functions. The data might relate to inputs (food consumed, supplements ingested, air quality), states (depth of sleep, mood, blood oxygen levels, blood pressure), or performance (mental or physical). It is often collected using devices, such as **fitness bands** and other **activity trackers**, **sleep monitors**, wifi-connected scales, and app-enabled smartphones. The amount and types of data collected will likely continue to grow along with the increasing use of **e-textiles** and **wearable sensors**.

The QS movement seeks to harness such data in order to improve one's health, performance, and longevity. Although QS approaches can be used, for example, to fine-tune a regimen of *nootropics,* this is not a fringe movement. Numerous firms ranging from *startups* to IBM (with its Watson system) are looking at ways to leverage **digital health** data. An interest in combating aging motivates many in the movement and across Silicon Valley. Alphabet's Calico looks to apply its larger sibling firm's experience analyzing data to this quest and the Palo Alto Longevity Prize *crowdsources* solutions.

The Quantified Self movement is not without detractors. Some healthcare professionals warn that unnecessary blood tests increase the chance of false positives, which can lead to unnecessary diagnoses and treatment. Moreover, it is possible that our ability to collect data has far surpassed our ability to properly interpret it, giving free reign to those peddling solutions to nonexistent problems.

Example sentences:

Since I've gotten into QS, I have lost weight and my insomnia is cured.

With three different fitness trackers and two different sleep monitors, I think he's gone a bit overboard with Quantified Self.

Based on data from her Quantified Self experimentation, she cut out nicotine and doubled down on caffeine.

Quotes:

"Members of the Quantified Self movement have invented bio-digital devices to track their daily calorie intake, alcohol intake, heart-rate, blood sugar levels, exercise regimes, social life, sex life, emotions, finances—there's even a digital rosary app to keep track of how many prayers you've said." — Jules Evans, Author, *Philosophy for Life and Other Dangerous Situations*

"There's no end to what people will attempt to measure ... People [are] thinking 'How can I quantify something I care about? How can I measure it and then use that measurement to do something with it?'" — Kevin Kelly, Owner, Cool Tools

"Today's medicine is more practice than science, albeit intelligent practice. Too much is left to qualitative judgments based on tradition, experience, and dated, often un-tested beliefs. But we are about to make a quantum leap in the capabilities of medicine driven by digital health technologies, sensors and data science. It's only a matter of time before this leap in technology empowers individuals to become the CEOs of their own health." — Vinod Khosla, Founder & Investment Partner, Khosla Ventures

"Ray Kurzweil might choke down 200 pills a day, but he's constantly getting blood work done and poring over the results. So my approach of performing a single liver test once a year wasn't looking too responsible, especially when other QS'ers were monitoring their blood sugar in real time for kicks." — Scott Jackisch, Principal, Globalize Networks

The Google Bus

The San Francisco Bay Area's two largest cities are at opposite ends of a peninsula separating the Bay from the Pacific Ocean. Just northwest of San Jose is Silicon Valley, overlapping with a stretch to the north often simply known as **the Peninsula**, and finally San Francisco at the upper tip. Many of the Bay Area's tech firms are in Silicon Valley and the Peninsula. While those area's cities are charming, they are rather suburban in feel, and lack the grit and energy of San Francisco or cities across the Bay such as Berkeley and Oakland. Many workers at technology firms, especially the younger ones, choose to live in those urban areas and commute to jobs on the Peninsula.

In an attempt to cater to this highly desirable workforce, and to enable them to be more productive during commuting time, many high tech firms in Silicon Valley have taken to running daily bus services, collectively referred to as **Google buses**, that ferry employees between home and work. The large buses are a phenomenon, standing out on city streets and leading to higher real estate prices near their arranged stops.

To their credit, the buses help the traffic situation by taking cars off the road, but as a conspicuous symbol of recent changes in the character of the City, they are also a target of resentment. The influx of highly-paid workers, in an area with already severe housing issues, has accelerated **gentrification**, revitalizing (some say) rundown neighborhoods but driving up rents and forcing middle- and lower-class residents from their homes. The buses, as symbols of this, have been targets of protests and vandalism.

The need for Google buses has been reduced somewhat as tech companies small and large have opened offices in San Francisco, but the underlying tensions remain.

Example sentences:

That apartment is expensive because it's near a Google bus stop.

Those Googlers come to San Francisco on their buses just to ruin everything that's great about the place.

He gets a lot of work done commuting with wifi on the Google bus.

Quotes:

"Nearly 40 companies operate the cushy, mostly unregulated coaches that make more [than] 200 stops a day—mainly in public bus zones—across the city. Google runs more than 100 buses that make 380 trips daily around the Bay Area." — *USA Today*

"About 69% of 'no-fault' housing evictions in San Francisco take place within four blocks of shuttle bus stops for tech employees, according to the Anti-Eviction Mapping Project, an online resource created by activists who are opposed to the gentrification of the city by wealthy tech workers." — Jim Edwards, Founding Editor, *Business Insider UK*

"Sometimes the Google Bus just seems like one face of Janus-headed capitalism; it contains the people too valuable even to use public transport or drive themselves." — Rebecca Solnit, Author, *Infinite City: A San Francisco Atlas*

"Last month, a group of gentrification protesters unleashed their rage on a piñata of a Google Bus, an act that seemed at once sadly impotent and uncomfortably close to violence." — James Temple, Senior Director, *The Verge*

"It's amusing at some level ... people are complaining that their nice cafe views are being ruined by Google Buses." — Ariel Waldman, Global Director, Science Hack Day

Burning Man

Every September, San Francisco becomes eerily quiet. Residents leave to attend **Burning Man**, an independent arts festival held each year in the desert of Nevada that attracts thousands of people.

The festival, with its emphasis on creativity and iconoclasm, is near and dear to people in Silicon Valley. Leaders and staff from many tech companies are regulars at Burning Man, where they get new ideas and make new connections in an environment completely different from everyday life. They wear costumes (or nothing at all), use pseudonyms, and eschew both money and the display of brands. Participants, called **Burners**, create massive art projects and other displays. They also bond in the difficult environment of the **playa** (flat desert basin, derived from the Spanish word for beach) where Burning Man is held, which is hot and dusty and prone to sandstorms, but is transformed into Black Rock City. The overall effect is one of camaraderie and stimulation in a setting that promotes new thinking. Burning Man's core principles were encoded in 2004 by Co-founder Larry Harvey as: radical inclusion; gifting; decommodification (anti-commercialism); radical self-reliance; radical self-expression; communal effort; civic responsibility; leaving no trace (avoid MOOP—matter out of place); participation; and immediacy.

Controversy, however, has emerged, as another aspect of the tech world now affects Burning Man: the rise of the moneyed elite. The titans of tech have begun to bring their wealth to bear in order to make Burning Man attendance more comfortable. They stay in private **plug and play camps** (which reduce the up-front planning required to attend) that include air-conditioned trailers and are set up and maintained by **sherpas** (a reference to the guides who support mountain climbers in the Himalayas) who are paid to relieve them from effort and pamper them with gourmet meals and massages. Many criticize such luxury and isolation as spoiling the spirit of the event.

Burning Man's ephemeral nature (epitomized by the conflagration for which it is named) contrasts with the organizers' purported plans to develop a year-round community based on the event.

Example sentences:

Burning Man sounds like fun, but I'm just not excited about spending a week being thirsty and dirty and trying to keep the sand out of my eyes.

I've been a Burner for the past ten years. I wouldn't miss it!

Every year, when the city empties out and it feels like everyone who is anyone is at Burning Man, I feel like I'm missing out.

Quotes:

"The tech scene has this sense that you can do anything, build anything, no rules—Burning Man is all about that, so it's a really conducive place for those conversations to start." — Molly Maloof, Physician and Strategy Advisor

"I really feel like Mike Judge has never been to Burning Man, which is Silicon Valley. If you haven't been, you just don't get it." — Elon Musk, CEO, Tesla Motors, Chairman & Co-founder, SolarCity and CEO & CTO, SpaceX

"The tech start-ups now go to Burning Man and eat drugs in search of the next greatest app. Burning Man is no longer a counterculture revolution. It's now become a mirror of society." — Tyler Hanson, Owner, Kulturehaus

"At some point, *not* going to Burning Man will be perceived as more hard-core than going, and I'll be way ahead of the curve." — Aaron Levie, CEO, Box

Index

About the Authors

Rochelle Kopp is a management consultant who works with global companies doing business in Silicon Valley, and Silicon Valley companies doing business globally. Her specialties include communication skills, leadership, cross-cultural management and human resource management. She frequently works with entrepreneurs and other businesspeople from overseas helping them to navigate the culture in Silicon Valley. She holds a BA in History from Yale University and an MBA from the University of Chicago.

Steven Ganz is the Founder of Teamifier, a startup to support collaborative, crowdsourced problem-solving. Steve has worked in Silicon Valley for over 10 years, both for startups and consulting to startups and research labs. In his consulting, Steve has helped clients plan, implement, validate, and/or promote their core technologies. He has a PhD in Computer Science (Programming Languages) from Indiana University and business and engineering degrees from the University of Pennsylvania's Wharton School and School of Engineering and Applied Science, respectively.

Please contact us at the following:

Email:
> Rochelle.Kopp@japanintercultural.com
> Steven.Ganz@genetius.com

Website: http://www.siliconvalleyspeak.com

Twitter: https://twitter.com/SVSpeak

Facebook: https://www.facebook.com/SiliconValleySpeak/

Instagram: https://www.instagram.com/SVSpeak/

Linkedin:
> https://www.linkedin.com/in/rochellekopp
> https://www.linkedin.com/in/stevenganz

For news about new Silicon Valley buzzwords and trends, please subscribe to our Valley Speak newsletter. Signup is at http://www.siliconvalleyspeak. com. At that site you will also find a fun quiz to test your knowledge of Silicon Valley jargon—we're hoping that after reading this book you will score a perfect ten!

Speaking and Consulting

Rochelle Kopp and Steven Ganz are available to speak to your group on the following topics:

- How to Talk Like a Silicon Valley Insider
- How to Speak Startup
- How Silicon Valley Innovates
- Getting Started in Silicon Valley
- Why Everyone Hates the Way Silicon Valley Talks
- The Culture of Silicon Valley
- Communicating Silicon Valley Style
- Managing People in Silicon Valley – Recruiting, Retention and HR Compliance
- Networking in Silicon Valley

We are also available to consult to entrepreneurs and established corporations coming to Silicon Valley on the following topics:

Communicate Silicon Valley Style!
Effective communication techniques for networking, pitches, meetings, and correspondence with potential investors, partners, collaborators and employees in Silicon Valley.

Hiring and Managing in Silicon Valley
The basics of hiring and managing people in the U.S., including how to find candidates, interview do's and don'ts, defining roles, creating job descriptions, managing performance, evaluations, and compensation. Special things to be aware of in California (which has particularly strict labor laws) and in Silicon Valley (which has a very competitive labor market) will also be covered.

Technical Communication for the Entrepreneur

How to discuss your business and technology with the sophistication and polish expected in Silicon Valley. How to express your ideas and respond to criticisms powerfully and succinctly.

Silicon Valley Tech Trends

Silicon Valley is an exciting place where technology is pushed to its limits and new industries based, for example, on artificial intelligence/machine learning, big data, cryptocurrency, or virtual reality seem to appear overnight. We will survey and discuss various of these technology trends, customized to your interests.

For further information please contact:

Rochelle.Kopp@japanintercultural.com or Steven.Ganz@genetius.com